D1294001

from

DIPLOMA

to

DREAM JOB

★ ★ ★ ★ ★

5 OVERLOOKED STEPS
TO A SUCCESSFUL CAREER

Beth Kuhel   **Mauri Artz**

Copyright © 2011 Beth Kuhel and Mauri Artz
All rights reserved.

ISBN: 1461087082
ISBN-13: 9781461087083
Library of Congress Control Number: 2011905996

TESTIMONIALS

"I co-founded the world's largest recruitment agency, Management Recruiters, International (MRI) and served as its CEO for 35 years. I have therefore been involved in relationships with tens of thousands of employers and even a higher number of candidates. Early on I recognized a certain gap in the dynamics that existed between recent college graduates (entry level) and employers. What I discerned and what exists today, is that these young people, coming out of college, are for the most part totally unprepared and incapable of presenting themselves properly to employers– and in fact,they cannot forge the kind of connectedness that is so necessary in this process.

This the first book of which I am aware, that bridges the gap that currently exists. The authors' backgrounds and experiences are admirably suited to the needs of the young people that they intend to reach through the publication of this book. In fact, they actually start with advice to the high school student and then move right into their college experience. They advise and then guide the student into an awareness of what they must do while still in school to bridge the gap that would otherwise stand between them and the position to which they aspire. They get into the meat of the matter, the concrete steps that must be taken, including even how the students should conduct themselves in an interview. There is also special attention paid to young women; also quite a bit of motivation and if you will, "self-help" of a very practical and valuable nature.

If a high school or a college student were to ask me what should be the first step toward ultimately going out into the world and getting the job they want-I would refer them to this book."

Alan R. Schonberg, Chairman Emeritus,
Management Recruiters International.

"Kuhel and Artz's "From Diploma to Dream Job" is an encyclopedia of tasks for those seeking an agile and upwardly mobile career path. The reader who follows the book's guideposts will find comfort that they are located in a geographic region that meets their lifestyle objectives while assuring their job search is not in the midst of ground zero for tomorrow's rust belt."

Rick Morgenstern Chairman and CEO,
Digital Authentication Technologies (Boca Raton, FL)

"From Diploma to Dream Job" was my personal career coach. I presented myself in a whole new light and found a CAREER instead of an hourly job."

Azra Kalic, Cleveland State University graduate

"You and your book taught me how to act in an interview and what and what not to say. You helped me feel relaxed and confident and I believe that eventually lead to my job offer. Your book also taught me how to structure my answers to interview questions to make them relevant to the field and office I was applying for.

You also took a look at my resume and helped me realize that it needs to be tailored to the type of job I am applying for. You also taught me how to use my resume as a guideline for what to talk about in my interviews. Speaking with you and just refreshing my mind on some of your tips in your book made me feel prepared and confident in any interview setting. I rocked my interview because of you and it eventually lead to me getting the job!"

Alexa Lefton, University of Wisconsin graduate

"The chapters on developing my brand and interviewing totally changed my perspective and gave me confidence. Thank you.

James Reynolds, University of Arizona graduate

"The concepts I learned from this book inspired me to create a personal mission statement early in my academic career, and this ultimately helped me to secure entry into a top university. I have networked with professors and have received several great opportunities for moving forward in my field by "minding the gatekeepers." I strongly recommend this book for any young person at the crossroads of these important decisions."

Galya Loeb, Northwestern University student

"This book offers very valuable information for young job seekers."

Terri Mrosko, Employment Column Freelance Writer, Cleveland Plain Dealer

---

"Wow! What a fabulous book this is. Where was this when my children were going through this process? I have read many how-to guides, but "From Diploma to Dream Job" has everything, from applying to the right college for you, to maximizing your college years, applying to graduate school and applying for your first job. This is definitely a cookbook – nothing is left out.

The authors have written lovingly from their own experiences, as well as from vast research on resume building, how to get your foot in the door, interviewing, networking, and pursuing flexible work option, and many other topics relevant to college, graduate school and career building. I particularly appreciated the section on different communities and what they may or may not offer to you, as an individual.

I have been in a position many times over when students have asked for my advice, and I wish I could have referred them to this book. It is so timely to offer this kind of advice to young people today in this economic climate."

Rochelle P. Ripple, Pd.D. Professor of Education Columbus State University, Division of the University of Georgia Columbus, GA

Thanks so much to our families and for all their support as we developed, researched, wrote and edited the book. We have had the privilege of speaking with countless students, working men and women, stay at home moms, hiring managers, university career counselors, college admissions officers, and high school college counselors. We thank each and every one of them for their helpful insights.

We appreciated the help of agent Laurie Harper for her guidance, and journalism student Emily Labes, who charmed us with her sense of humor and youthful style. We appreciate the work of Snowbelt Designs on our cover, as well as generational marketing expert Cam Marston, whose insights greatly aided our understanding.

To our husbands, Alan and Philip, thanks for your patience. We are grateful for our parents, who taught us the importance of education and developing our skills to positively impact the lives of others.

This book is dedicated to our children, Ryan and Tali Kuhel, and Max, Carson, Cassidy and Annie Artz. You inspired us to write a helpful book for you and your generation. Thank you.

BK and MA

Table of Contents:

About the Authors:

Beth Kuhel has 25 years of experience in marketing, sales, strategic planning, personnel management, and recruiting. She was retained by both non-profit and for profit organizations ranging from the computer industry to active travel and educational institutions, to draft and revise their marketing plans. Beth received her BA with distinction from the University of Michigan and attended their graduate program in business before completing her MBA at George Washington University. In the last few years, Beth has dedicated herself to extensively researching trends in hiring to provide timely, accessible, and useful information for students and graduates developing career plans.

Mauri Artz runs her own test preparation business for college-bound students. She is also retained by private schools to provide in-house coaching on college entrance exams as well as college admissions essays. Mauri has worked as a corporate attorney, a corporate editor, a clerk in federal court, and has written for online travel magazines. She received her JD from Case Western Reserve University School of Law and was a Wigmore Scholar at Northwestern University School of Law. She received her BA summa cum laude from Tulane University.

Introduction: How to Best Utilize This Book:

This guide is filled to the brim with advice and tools that apply to several junctures in the academic and/or career path. Although each chapter may be viewed independently, collectively all the chapters are meant to offer a "big picture" methodology to help you find and land your dream job and position in life. The purpose of this book is to alleviate the stress of this difficult economy and to give you some concrete processes to follow as you navigate your way through it. Although you should read the chapters that specifically apply to where *you* are in your life most carefully, it would be beneficial to read the whole book in order to understand each chapter in context.

TO THE YOUNG ADULT:

If you purchased this book for yourself, we assume that you are about to enter the realm of college, graduate school, or your first job. You've probably seen many books about each of these monumental transitions. This book is special because unlike most guides of its kind, it was written with the intent to help you through *every* transition you'll face in your young adult life. We want to be your companion for the next five years, ten years, and beyond!

You may still be trying to answer the age-old question, "What do I want to do when I grow up?" Our goal is to help you answer this question for *yourself*. This guidebook is designed to help you face the tough decisions now that will lead to a fulfilling life in the long run. Remember: This is your life, these are your dreams, and this is your world. We hope this book will give you the structure and strategies you'll need to face the challenges of today's economy and the world in general.

TO THE PARENTS OF YOUNG ADULTS:

If you bought this book for your young adult, then you have made a wise investment. We urge you to guide your children to make their own well-reasoned, well-researched decisions in life, rather than the decisions they feel would please *you*. In fact, if you take too much ownership of this process, you'll essentially take away your child's emerging power. This is not to say that you shouldn't help your children by opening doors, asking pertinent questions, and offering unwavering support. As Malcolm Gladwell noted in his bestseller *Outliers*, "No one—not rock stars, not professional athletes, not software billionaires, and not even geniuses—ever make it alone." As parents, you supply your children with abundant resources. However, the willingness to explore and utilize these resources must come from them.

This book explains the processes, provides the research, and outlines the tools to help you navigate one of the most important journeys of your life. Success is a result of many combined variables. Formal education is important. Yet emotional intelligence, mindfulness of individuals you encounter along the way, and your ability to utilize the unique attributes of your circumstances will all empower you to make the right decisions.

A NEW WORKPLACE, A NEW GAME PLAN:

In a world with staggering unemployment rates and an economy that goes up and down like a yo-yo, it's safe to say that the job markets of our mothers and fathers have effectively vanished. Needless to say, things have changed. In order to combat these changes, we need a new, innovative approach to tackle these tough issues related to entering college, graduate school, and the job market. This book is intended to help today's generation of young people find their way to a rewarding career despite the seemingly desperate economic climate. Use this book as a compass to help point you in the right direction as you embark on this journey. We speak directly to *you* because only YOU can take the responsibility to navigate the waters of your life.

In reading this book, you'll learn how to address the current challenges all young people face. You'll specifically be advised on how to get into a certain college and/or how to land a specific job; how to approach the journey of choosing a career and a lifestyle that is obtainable, realistic, and will ultimately make you happy. The opportunity to make great choices for your future will depend on the possession of information about the marketplace you'll be entering. You can also gain insight into your future based on the wisdom of those who have made great choices and found happiness in both their personal and professional lives. This guide will provide you with an easy-to-follow methodology for finding happiness in your career and will ultimately help to reduce stress along the way. So say "good-bye" to sleepless nights and incessant migraines! We hope you will discover that the more information you have, the more excited you will become about riding off into the sunset of your future.

IF YOU ARE IN HIGH SCHOOL:

Although you are most likely up to your neck in college applications, statements of purpose, and personal entrance essays, be sure to take some time to step back and look out into the horizon. *You must plan further ahead than the next four years of your life.* College is expensive and student loans can add up quickly. It will pay off in the long run to begin asking yourself questions *now* about where you want to end up in five years. Take the time to stop and assess your interests and career goals.

The point is: Take the time to think not just about getting through college, but instead where you want to be in four years. The decisions you're about to make (i.e. what college to attend and what subject to major in) will have a great impact on your job search in four years. It's not too early to read this book. Nearly all of the principles and advice set forth here can be followed right away.

IF YOU ARE IN COLLEGE:

We would like to start by telling you what this book is *not*. It is not a pitch to choose a career path that earns you the most amount of money with the least amount of work. Instead, this is a rational guide to help you on your quest to find satisfaction in whatever you choose to do after college. *This guide should be used as a practical set of tools and advice to help you land the life – not just the job – that you have always wanted and that will make you happy.*

This book is not at all meant to limit your career options. Instead, it is a call to explore all of your options and investigate new and exciting areas of work that may provide the fertile soil for many fulfilling job options. Maybe you'll choose to begin work in a particular field while pursuing an advanced degree. Perhaps you'll find a city that you will fall in love with and an exciting industry that you never considered entering. The avenues you can travel in life are endless.

At this point in your life, your future success and overall happiness will largely be determined by the amount of investigation and personal reflection you do right now. You must learn to develop and use your *practical intelligence*, a concept that will be defined and discussed throughout the book. Practical intelligence is the ability to look into the future and see what your needs, desires, and passions are in order to make the right decisions now. This book will help show you *what* you should be investigating, *how* to ask pertinent questions, *learn* from these questions, and ultimately to *look before you leap!*

IF YOU ARE IN GRADUATE SCHOOL:

It is now time to make your higher education start paying dividends! What you will gain from this guide will be invaluable advice for finding, landing, and building not only a great career, but also a healthy and fulfilling life. Remember: There are many factors that contribute to a lifestyle of contentment, not just a lucrative career.

You will also benefit from at least considering moving to a city that is showing signs of sustainability in job potential. You should at least investigate the city's character and consider whether or not it offers a viable lifestyle for you. This book is not attempting to push you in one direction or another. It is instead intended to guide you in making these important decisions. You are looking not only for a job, but also for a way of life.

We hope to help clarify *your* plan for *your* life by guiding you through each step of the process. You must clarify your objectives and ask yourself questions like:

- What do I expect out of my career?
- What type of lifestyle do I envision for myself?
- Are there job options I have *not* considered that may utilize my education and skills?

The more of these questions that you think about and answer now, the better prepared you will be for the work of building not only your career but also a pleasurable life.

YOU HAVE YOUR COLLEGE DIPLOMA IN HAND... SO WHAT NEXT?

These days, guidebooks for getting into college or grad school are a dime a dozen. Yet where are the books about what happens *after* you earn your degree and begin that difficult, and sometimes downright scary, task of looking for a job? What do you do when Monster.com doesn't have a single job you are qualified (or perhaps over-qualified) for? This could be the most difficult transitional period of your life; you shouldn't have to face it unprepared.

While many parents assume that their children will settle in the places where they were raised, many graduates find themselves moving to large, metropolitan areas, hoping for an increased chance of finding work. Although we highlight areas that are experiencing growth in this turbulent economic climate, this is not meant to be a definitive last word on *the place to be* during the next decade. Instead, *we have written this book as a structured, low-anxiety sourcebook—a pocket guide, if you will—for anyone who is asking the question, "So, what next?"* Our pocket guide is set up to help you make thoughtful, practical decisions about a career path and ultimately where you want to settle down to live. Never has there been such a large body of college graduates facing such a difficult job market and thus such difficult decisions. We are here to give you a helping hand with the tough decisions that lie ahead.

FINDING "HOT PLACES TO LIVE AND WORK":

One way to approach this daunting phase of your life is to shift your focus to the *places* that offer not only the possibility of steady employment, but are also attracting an emerging talent base to create new, well-paying jobs. In other words, look for places that seem to be alive with new industries, a large influx of young talent, and a strong base of people working in professional occupations. We have spent quite some time researching areas that fit this description and display this sort of potential.

More importantly, we have tried to capture the *personality* of these cities in terms of quality of life, which is an aspect of job hunting that should not be neglected. A thorough investigation of a potential move to a big city (or anywhere, for that matter) is essential for anyone considering moving away from his or her hometown. This is not a decision that should be taken lightly.

Remember: A city brimming with vitality in one working sector could be on life support in another industry. You also need to find the *city personality* that is compatible with your own personality. So what is the key to figuring out where to move in order to land a great job? Do your research. Investigate.

Assess the "flavor" of a city, the viability of your sector in the city, and the amount of opportunities available for you to meet your career and personal goals. You could view the assessment as a type of business plan. Develop your own *mission statement* that maps out what you want from life, and then periodically refer to that statement by asking yourself: Are my college major, internship, summer employment, career aspirations, location for training, and first job in sync with my mission? If the answer is, "yes," then keep moving forward with that plan. If you see a conflict between your personal mission statement and the choices you are making: *Stop* and re-evaluate. Maybe you need to alter your mission statement or take a different turn with the education, training, and jobs you are pursuing. Businesses do this all the time. The wonderful thing is: you are in the driver's seat now and you have youth and ambition in your favor.

The best time to make a change in your career path is now. *Don't be a person who is easily persuaded or goes wherever the wind blows. Be in charge of your own life.* There are plenty of unhappy people who pursued careers because their parents, peers, older siblings, etc. pushed them in a certain direction. These miserable individuals still blame the people who misadvised them for their own poor choices.

We happen to know a certain individual who went to graduate school and landed a high-paying job as a financial director of a bank. He was miserable for twenty years. Why? His real passion was marketing, and rather than follow his own intuition, he was subconsciously fulfilling his parents' dream. Was he happy that he had a job? Yes. Did he maximize his professional ability and personal happiness? No.

A COLLEGE GRADUATE'S TOOLBOX FOR THE NEXT STEP:

As you weave your "next step" tapestry, you will find yourself in need of some tools to get the job done. Consider this book your own personal "tool box" that contains suggestions for many skills you should develop including:

- **Resume building**
- **How to get your foot in the door**
- **Interviewing**
- **Networking**
- **Pursuing flexible working options**

Ultimately we hope that in reading this book you will gain pragmatic information and advice concerning your hunt for a meaningful career.

What becomes obvious throughout this book is the fact that you must begin to reflect on what *you* really want out of life. Once you *"know thyself"* you will realize that this is not just a job search, but also a major step toward defining and obtaining the life you wish to lead.

At your stage of the game, this whole discussion may sound crazy. You may be saying to yourself, "I sound so full of myself and insincere. No way am I saying this stuff." The truth of the matter is that you are crossing over to the real world now, and in the real world, you are the one who knows your strengths the best. You must seek to understand your strengths and to share them with potential colleges and potential employers. Rabbi Hillel, a famous biblical scholar, once said something like, "If I am not for myself, who will be for me? But if I am only for myself, who am I?" His words have such lasting meaning, no wonder we are still quoting him thousands of years later! You are entering a world where adults are making decisions that will impact your life—so you must teach yourself to communicate in a way that adults understand. You must try to learn to be self-confident and strong without coming off as arrogant and insincere.

Although you may grow physically ill at the thought of doing *homework* after so many years in school, doing a little homework now is a wise and inexpensive investment in your future. Having a plan about your future can save you not only a lot of money toward moving expenses, it can also spare you the costs involved with the life disruption that will inevitably occur every time you switch jobs or locations.

In many ways, you become married to the job you choose, your employer, and your city. DO NOT enter this marriage without the advice and tools presented in this guide. Similar to a divorce, moving to a different job or city can be costly, time-consuming, and stressful – no matter how much happier it makes you in the long run.

So here is the point: you have the opportunity now to ask yourself difficult questions about career life and to learn where to find the answers. *This book aims to abolish that far-too-common quote we hear from so many middle-aged people:* "If only I had known then what I know now."

We are going to let you in on the *secrets* that we learned through our own trial and error as well as the experiences of others. Our intent is for *you* to learn from *our* mistakes as well as our successes. In order for you to benefit from the information in this book, you will need to learn how to ask yourself the right questions at the right times. Only you can provide these answers, but we can help you to see what the best questions are given the situation. This inquiry and introspection will be well-secured investments in your future.

Throughout your journey, we will continue to urge you to ask yourself the "difficult questions." The reason these questions are deemed "difficult" is because you have probably spent many years answering them based on what you think others expect of you. You must begin to do some soul searching as soon as possible! By choosing to read this book, you have already demonstrated a high level of emotional intelligence. Use the strategies and advice in this book to move your career—and your life—forward. Eventually this will allow you to reach the goals you have set for yourself.

In the bestselling book *Outliers*, Malcolm Gladwell highlights people who have accomplished amazing feats in their lifetimes. From Gladwell's fascinating prose, we learn that these "Outliers" find success by knowing how to harness and utilize the particulars of their circumstances that will aid them in reaching their goals. For some, this is ancestry or legacy; for others, it is mentors and friendships. Many times success is determined by the idiosyncrasies of particular selection processes used to identify talent. Why not learn all you can about the processes that will be used to determine your admission to schools or your suitability for a particular job?

STEP 1

STEP 1:

Know what you bring to the table and what drives you.

 **Opening the First Door: What to Do in High School and As You Enter College**

Despite what movies like *The Breakfast Club* seem to indicate, life does not end after high school graduation. In fact, high school is just the beginning! It is *not* too early to begin planning your life and considering your potential career while you're still in high school. In fact, this stage in your life is a great time to make a plan about where you want to be in ten or twenty years. *If you know where you want to be in the future, you can create strategies that will help you to accomplish your goals.* The information in this chapter will teach you how to make the most of your high school experience while preparing yourself for life after you don your cap and gown.

ACADEMICS: FOCUS ON MORE THAN JUST YOUR GRADES!

You should begin by building a strong, positive relationship with your college guidance counselor. Your counselor is a human resource whose goal is to help *you* succeed. Don't wait until you're a senior to talk to that person about college—seek him or her out at some point in your freshman year to talk about your future plans. Beginning to focus on your future as early as freshman year will give you a leg up early in the game.

Perhaps you might consider making a four-year plan with regard to your high school classes. Think ahead as much as possible and try to figure out which classes you will take each year of high school. You may want to do research in advance to figure out which Honors and Advanced Placement (AP) courses will be available to you in the future and whether or not the latter will count for college credit. AP classes offer an exam at the end that, if passed, awards you a few college credits.

Taking a few college courses throughout your high school career might not be a bad idea either. Some students opt to take a college-level course in a subject that interests them during their senior year. The advantages of such a venture are abundant. If you're a mature student, it will be beneficial for you to be exposed to a college environment. Taking college-level courses will also help you to stand out when it comes time to fill out college applications. Then of course there are the extra credits you will accrue. Taking the courses in high school can also help you to save money once you arrive in college. Your school counselor should be able to answer any questions you have in this department.

You might also consider taking a gap year between high school and college. In recent years, this route has become very popular. A plethora of programs are available to help make sure that you use your gap year wisely. If you take a gap year, your aim is to return to school more mature, settled, focused, and ready to buckle down. Many students find that after high school, they need a year to become acclimated with the real world in order to grow and mature enough to be ready for college. If you feel that you would benefit from such a year, don't be ashamed. Recognizing the need for growth is, in fact, a sign of wisdom rather than immaturity. Many colleges recognize this and look favorably upon it. If finances are tight, ask your guidance counselor to assist you in finding scholarship money. You may be surprised how many study abroad programs offer financial aid. Just Google studyabroad.com and you'll find a list of organizations offering support.

As important as it is to plan ahead, remember to also make sure your grades are still a priority. Devote yourself to your schoolwork and don't be afraid to ask for help when you need it. Older peer tutors and teachers—as intimidating as you may find them—are usually available to help students who care enough to ask for help or clarification. *One bad grade will not ruin your life, but you should still try to earn the best grades possible.* Do extra credit, revise your papers, attend study sessions, etc. You don't have to present your teachers with shiny red apples in order to show that you care. Remember: If there is help out there, then by all means, take advantage of it!

EXTRACURRICULAR ACTIVITIES – A REWARDING WAY TO INVEST IN YOUR FUTURE:

The extracurricular activities you choose to do indicate a great deal about your character as well as your aspirations. Start by asking yourself, "What do I love to do?" Then find activities that are academic, athletic, service-oriented, or fine arts related (for example) and investigate how to get involved in the area of your choice. You don't have to be the starting quarterback or the star goalie in order to look good to the colleges to which you apply!

If you love science, inquire about research or lab opportunities or enter a science fair. If math is your passion, perhaps there's a math challenge team or club that you could participate in. Literary magazines, school newspapers, and working on the yearbook provide great opportunities for aspiring writers or photojournalists. School plays, orchestras, choral groups, and dance teams might be the route to take for the aspiring performance artist. Political campaigns, student government, and the debate team might satisfy the future politicians of the world. High school is a veritable paradise for indulging in your passions, whatever they may be.

We also recommend using your free time to volunteer. There are many ways to find volunteer opportunities. Your guidance counselors and teachers are often aware of great ways to get involved in the school as well as the community at large. Network with your parents' friends and contacts. A number of websites are devoted to helping people find places to volunteer. A few include:

- volunteermatch.com
- networkforgood.com
- idealist.com
- friendshipcircle.com

Be sure to keep track of all of your volunteer hours and experiences. You may want to keep a journal or use an online hours tracker such as the one available at www.presidentialserviceawards.gov.

You should also consider pursuing a non-paying internship. Even in high school, internships offer valuable insight into potential careers. *Use any professional experience you can, whether it lasts for a week or a summer, to learn about career paths that interest you.* Whether your passion is retail, law, medicine, government, technology, environmental science, doing back handsprings while singing the French national anthem, or any other area or activity, take the initiative to become informed about your possible career path.

At this point, it would be a good idea for you to begin looking through books, such as *The Fiske Guide to Colleges,* to become familiar with the specialties of certain colleges and what programs they offer. Talk to the college recruiters who visit your high school about programs of study you find interesting. Give yourself a competitive edge in high school by taking the time to become aware of the many careers associated with your areas of interest.

One of the major obstacles in career planning is figuring out which of the millions of jobs available in this country to research. The U.S. Department of Labor states that there are more than 12,000 job opportunities available in the United States at any given time. Later, we will discuss in depth possible career paths based on possible areas of study.

NAILING THE STANDARDIZED TESTS:

These tests are often critical in the application process even as many schools begin to minimize their importance. Therefore you should engage in activities that will help you to expand both your vocabulary and your critical thinking skills. You should read, write, and brush up on basic math skills and participate in lab sciences to keep these areas sharp. Taking these tests will be far less daunting if you've been preparing throughout high school.

If your high school offers practice SAT and ACT tests (this varies from school to school), you should take advantage of them. Prepare for these actual tests as though they are the real tests. Websites such as collegeboard.com and act.org offer practice questions and tests. Many public libraries offer free courses on test taking, and a variety of books on test preparation are available to help you master the strategies. It might also be beneficial to hire a professional tutor to assist you in your preparation or to take a specialized test prep course if your finances allow. Older, successful students can also provide a great deal of help in this area.

RECOGNIZE AND RESPECT THE GATEKEEPERS:

A gatekeeper is a person who you encounter during high school that will play some role in controlling the gates that either open to you or remain closed. Here is a list of just some examples of gatekeepers with whom you will be interacting over the course of the next four years:

- **Parents:** They may be paying part or all of your college tuition. For most students, parents are the most important supporting cast members.

- **College representatives:** These individuals visit your school and will talk to you about opportunities their schools can give you. Often they are the people who will read over your applications.

- **Employers and references from volunteer work:** If you've made an impact somewhere, you will be remembered. The impression you make may help or hurt you in the future.

- **Guidance counselors:** They stand at the gate of college and post-graduate opportunities. They can also provide college letters of recommendation for you.

- **Teachers:** By writing letters of recommendation or opening other doors for you in terms of service, volunteering, award nominations, or extra help, your teachers have a strong impact on your future.

Of course, you may find gatekeepers in many other realms as well—be sure to keep an eye out for them. As this section's title indicates, treat them with respect. When these gatekeepers take the time to see or help you, be sure to send thank you notes to show your gratitude. Be on time to your meetings with them and if you are requesting their help (i.e. a letter of recommendation) make sure you give them plenty of time to get it done. Network with the gatekeepers and make them your "allies for success." Here are a few sample thank you notes to help give you an idea of what yours should look like. Your notes should either be handwritten or sent via e-mail.

Dear _____,

Thank you very much for taking the time to meet with me (or: write a letter of recommendation for me). Your insights provided me with a great deal of information about _____

_____. I greatly appreciate your time, concern, and efforts. Your input will be of great value and I appreciate your willingness to help. Thank you again. I would be happy to assist you in the future, should the need arise.

Best,

Your name

Dear _____,

I want to let you know how much I appreciated our meeting today. Thank you for taking the time to explain (or: discuss) the dynamics/parameters of the _____ position in such detail. The more I learn about_____, the more excited I become about the possibility of joining such a dynamic organization. Thanks again for your time and consideration. I hope to hear from you soon (if applicable).

Best,

Your name

If you plan to have a personal interview at a college, take the time to prepare and practice in order to make yourself stand out. Here are some tips to help you make a great first impression with the colleges of your choice:

- Allow adequate time to prepare your college applications and proofread meticulously. Admissions officers welcome essays that display your voice and sincerely reflect your personality.
- Be able to discuss your strengths, passions, accomplishments, and—in some cases—your weaknesses.
- Be ready to elaborate on why you would be a "great fit" for the school and what you can add to the community of learners. Note: being able to chug five beers in one minute is *not* an impressive prerequisite.

- Keep in mind that some interviewers may ask questions about books, events, people, etc. that have influenced you. Be ready to answer them.
- Learn as much as you can about the university before the interview. Be prepared to explain why you're interest in the school, whether it's because of a specific program, stellar sports teams, a sterling reputation, etc.

When the interviewer asks if you have any questions, always respond by asking thoughtful questions that further indicate who you are.

When you apply to colleges, it's important to know what each school is looking for in their potential students, particularly in terms of character traits. Admissions offices are not just looking for a well-written response (although your response must be well crafted); they are interested in who you are as a person. Some attractive traits that you should try to display are: adaptability, leadership, and composure when faced with stress or failure.

Below are some actual college entrance essay questions from some of the most prestigious universities in the country. Practice answering these questions and always ask yourself, "By asking this question, what do they hope to learn about me?" While reading the questions we provide, your goal should be to think about *your* life and how you can start to build a foundation *now* that will allow you to confidently answer these questions. Get a head start on "packaging yourself" as this will give you the competitive edge you will need later in life. It's never too early to contemplate how to address these topics. If you find yourself unable to answer some of these questions, ask yourself how you should pursue your passions in ways that will enable you to answer them in the future. Don't fear this process—engage and take control of it. As you read on, you will learn many ways to research, investigate, and discover your inner strengths.

FROM UNDERGRADUATE APPLICATIONS:

- Tell us about a time when you built or developed a team whose performance exceeded expectations.
- Tell us about a time when you made a lasting impact on an organization or group.
- Tell us about a time when you motivated others to support your vision or initiative.
- Tell us about a time when you went beyond what was defined, established, or expected.
- What are your career aspirations? How will your education at this university help you achieve them?
- What matters most to you, and why?

FROM GRADUATE SCHOOL APPLICATIONS:

- As a leader in global business, our school is committed to sustaining "a truly global presence through its engagement in the world." What goals are you committed to and why? How do you envision this MBA contributing to the attainment of these goals?
- Describe a failure that you have experienced. What role did you play, and what did you learn about yourself?
- Discuss how you have engaged with a community or organization.
- Give us a specific example of a time when you solved a complex problem.

- Master classes are the epitome of bridging the gap between theory and practice at the business school. Please provide an example from your own life in which practical experience taught you more than theory alone.
- Provide an example of a team failure of which you have been a part. If given a second chance, what would you do differently?
- Tell us about a time when you had to adapt by accepting/understanding the perspective of people different from yourself.
- Tell us about a time when you made a difficult decision.
- Tell us about something significant that you have done to improve yourself in either your professional and/or personal endeavors.
- What are your short-term and long-term post-MBA goals? How will this business school help you to achieve these goals?
- What are your three most substantial accomplishments and why do you view them as such?
- What have you learned from a mistake?
- What is your career vision, and why is this choice meaningful to you?
- What would you like the MBA admissions board to know about your undergraduate academic experience?
- Write a cover letter introducing yourself to the admissions board.

In responding to the above questions, always make sure your answers portray your best character traits. In chapter five you will be introduced to the concept of *how to positively portray negative traits*. This is a valuable skill. For instance, if you are someone who occasionally gets burnt out, you could talk about your untamable drive and dedication. Perhaps you find yourself often doing all the work on group presentations. It would be wise to discuss a time when you realized that you simply could not do all of the work by yourself and instead decided to delegate various portions of it to your workgroup while managing to inspire them. This shows that you overcame your over-active drive and learned how to be an effective and motivational leader as well as a teammate while maintaining enthusiasm for your work. An anecdote such as this one would also show that rather than avoiding difficult challenges, you meet them head on in a mature and professional fashion.

You should also make sure to demonstrate your *practical intelligence*-also known as *social* intelligence. We will discuss this concept in depth in chapter four. However, understand that social intelligence allows you to read between the lines and deduct what the question is *really* asking. Even a question about the size of your school can mask a deeper question. For instance, a student who chooses to stay at a small high school uses the opportunity to become involved in a plethora of activities and assumes leadership roles that he or she otherwise would not have the opportunity to explore in a larger institution. Choosing to become actively involved and attempting to effect change in the school can demonstrate (assuming one was effective) the ability to influence one's surroundings positively.

The interviewers/admissions committee are looking for certain qualities. Help them understand who you are by sharing an example. Don't just weigh the pros and cons of attending a small high school. The admissions office is *really* asking you how you were able to thrive in a fairly sheltered and close-knit environment. In addition, be aware that college admissions officers are trying to gauge your competence as a student as well as an individual who can function in a diverse group environment.

THE 10,000-FOOT VIEW, OR THINKING OUTSIDE OF THE BOX:

There are many other matters to consider when applying to college. For example, do you think you might be interested in postgraduate work, i.e. getting your master's and/or Ph.D.? If at this point you haven't thought that far ahead, don't be alarmed, you still have time to decide. However, if grad school is something that appeals to you, perhaps you should consider a less expensive undergraduate college or university so you can reserve some funds for graduate school. Once in college, you should keep in mind that while nachos at two in the morning may seem like a good idea, your wallet and your waistline would beg to differ.

You also might want to consider a double major in order to make the most of your college education. True, this could require more hours spent diligently studying at the library in the wee hours of the morning, but the benefits are invaluable. By majoring in more than one area, you will develop great variety in your skill set and expertise. Academic minors can also help you acquire a diverse set of skills. When you graduate college and start looking for a job in the "real world," that extra major or minor could give you the necessary flair to dazzle your prospective employers. Having two majors (or a minor) could also open up other fields of industry that might otherwise be closed to you. You are still developing as a student and a person. Thus be aware that it's not unusual to be uncertain about your major even once you're in college. Take advantage of all your educational opportunities. Over time, you will gravitate to an area where you will thrive.

Another factor to take into consideration before you embark on the wonderful quest we call the college process is the geographical location of the universities to which you are applying. Ask yourself:

- Will I be near a hot hiring epicenter in the field I eventually want to break into?
- Will traveling to and from school be too difficult?
- Will I be too far away from home?
- Do I *want* to be far away from home?

You may only spend four years in the city or town in which you go to school, but you should still feel at home there.

 # HOW TO MAXIMIZE COLLEGE

Some of the great advantages of a college education are the connections that you make along the way. Are there people at the university that you wish to attend who will serve as good connections and eventually help you network? Take advantage of every opportunity that becomes available to you. Your professors may only teach part-time and hold full-time jobs elsewhere in the business world. Get to know them. Often these enlightened individuals are a part of great social and professional networks that can provide you with terrific opportunities. They may also be willing to write letters of recommendation for you. Help your professors in any way possible. You could offer to grade papers, tutor students, or even get involved with their research. Note: you are not expected to pick up their dry-cleaning or walk their dogs.

For example, if you are passionate about literature and/or writing, get involved with the school's literary magazine. Then develop a professional relationship with the magazine's faculty advisor. The professor might be aware of available jobs in journalism or opportunities to work at other literary magazines. If you prove yourself to be a capable and intelligent individual while working with these guru-like guides, it's perfectly acceptable to ask, "Would you be willing to write me a letter of recommendation?" Express your gratitude for the professor's time and assistance. His or her referrals and letters of recommendation could make a big difference in your job hunt.

It's also important to look into the career services and alumni support that a college offers. How successful is your prospective college at helping students find employment upon graduation? Does the school offer resume workshops, mock interviews, etc.? All of these resources will aid you tremendously when you begin to look for a job after graduating or even if you choose to apply to a graduate program.

Surprisingly, choosing the right college for you may not translate into choosing the highest-ranked college that accepts you. In fact, there is a trend toward hiring graduates of large public institutions, according to recent studies by the *Wall Street Journal*. One recent *WSJ* study surveyed almost five hundred of the nation's largest public and private companies, government agencies, and nonprofits, and the results show that more entry-level jobs go to large state universities. Specifically, ten of the top twenty-five schools were public, only one of them an Ivy. The *WSJ's* study surveyed corporate recruiters, who in many cases must be selective with their visits due to economic restraints. Often companies focus on schools in neighboring locations to foster research relationships with professors. Many recruiters note the strength of students who develop strong critical thinking and communication skills in elite colleges. However, particularly in areas of business and engineering, companies are looking for students with top-notch practical skills that are often honed in the programs of large public universities.

The *Wall Street Journal* reported that the recruiters polled for their study represented companies that collectively hired forty-three thousand new students in 2009. According to the study, the recruiters pointed to the well-rounded academic preparation of students from top public universities, the ability of these students to fit into corporate cultures, and not surprisingly, the strong track records of these new hires at their respective firms. Again, employers are extremely interested in relationships with school professors, allowing many opportunities for students to obtain early internships and job opportunities.

When you are researching a school or a university for undergraduate or graduate work, ask which companies recruit or offer internship programs on a particular campus. You should also ask whether there are any research connections between the school and any large companies. In addition to the research connection with universities, many large companies have opened branches near popular colleges. For example, Google has opened an office near the University of Michigan in Ann Arbor as well as near Carnegie Mellon University in Pittsburgh. Locating near a college or university provides the company with a steady stream of interns and potential hires that do not have to relocate. When students interact with companies, there is instant brand awareness on campus that companies hope will translate into many talented new hires.

A recent article in the *Wall Street Journal* details just how valuable a college diploma may be. The *WSJ* reports on a study done by the College Board that cites college graduates as earning 60 percent more than those who have only graduated high school, on average, both annually and over the course of a lifetime. The article also describes a new online calculator tool, called Salary Calculator, that plugs in tests scores, schools attended, grades, and majors, and then generates a ten-year estimate of range of income post-college. The data is based on private and public sources and the reporting of actual graduates. Beyond salary, however, higher education provides many other intangible benefits. For example, some research suggests that college graduates show greater rates of civic participation. As previously mentioned, the innumerable amount of networking opportunities that you may gain during college often help in opening a variety of doors after graduation. General satisfaction in life is also something to be gained with a college degree. The Pew Research Center reports that college graduates have a 12 percent higher likelihood of claiming to be "very happy" in comparison to those who have only finished high school.

Interestingly enough, the *WSJ* also reports that another strong indicator of future income may be the caliber of schools that a student has *applied* to but not necessarily attended. In this study, students who applied to elite schools but did not attend them earned higher incomes than the actual attendees of said elite schools. The National Bureau of Economic Research concludes that, "evidently, students' motivation, ambition, and desire to learn have a much stronger effect on their subsequent success than average academic ability of their classmates." In other words, you do not have to attend an Ivy League school to have an Ivy League work ethic!

Remember, you are an incredibly powerful individual; YOU are in control of your future. First of all, relax and take a deep breath. Remaining calm and collected helps to reduce stress, which helps to increase success exponentially. Spend these next few years wisely cultivating important relationships, investigating your areas of interest, getting involved in your school as well as your community at large, and striving to achieve high grades and test scores. In a few years, all of the hard work you are doing now will pay off.

Even when you take all the right steps and do "all the right things," your best-layed plans do not always result in a victory. In some ways, you may have your first taste of the real world with a rejection letter or a callback that never comes. Perhaps you experienced rejection as you applied to highly selective colleges or graduate schools. Although your world seems crushed at the time, you shouldn't fear that disaster looms. In fact, the evidence points in the other direction. Many extraordinary people found the inner strength to carry on and eventually reach even greater success.

Perhaps one of the most poignant examples of rejection turnaround can be seen in the case of billionaire investor Warren Buffett. He was rejected by Harvard Business School and enrolled in Columbia Business School instead. At Columbia, he credits two of his professors with teaching him the investment principles that guided his success. Buffett qualifies that, with the exception of health issues, temporary defeats are not permanent ones. In an interview, Buffett suggests, "The truth is, everything that has happened in my life...that I thought was a crushing event at the time has turned out for the better."

Many high achievers, including Harold Varmus, winner of the Nobel Prize in Medicine, Scott McNealy, the co-founder of Sun Microsystems, Bill Gates, founder of Microsoft, Steve Jobs, head of Apple, Ted Turner, billionaire philanthropist, and film director Steven Spielberg, all report facing rejections that later propelled them to even greater successes. The general suggestion from all of these stories is that you have the power to take these rejections and to turn them into something positive. You may take rejection and use it to infuse you with the energy that you need to help you find your way. Your parents or family friends may open the door to reach one of these contact people. If that is the case, you are very fortunate. It's up to you, however, to take the next step. Decide what you need to know to help you figure out if this is the right path for you. It's crucial to know whether this is the right direction for you in terms of the day-to-day responsibilities the job will entail, the demands of the position, and the type of lifestyle it will provide.

Keep in mind that your purpose is twofold: to get information about this type of career and to figure out the best way to get there. You must be prepared on both fronts. The world is full of specialists. The more information you can gather about specialized areas, the more prepared you will be when it comes time for the true job interview. Although you should not offer your resume, it's a good idea to always carry a copy with you. This way, if the person you are interviewing asks for it, you'll be ready to present it. Below is a list of helpful questions to consider asking the person whom you choose to interview. If you don't have time to pose every question, choose the ones that are most important to you.

- When did you decide to follow this career path?
- Can you trace the course of your development? School? Mentors? Family? Networking?
- What mistakes did you make along the way and what decisions do you look back on favorably?
- Can you describe the career path which led you to this position?
- Which attributes would you consider the most directly related to your success in reaching this level in your firm?
- Can you describe the corporate culture of your firm?
- Who were your mentors and how did you acquire them? How were they helpful to you?
- What would you say are the bonuses, perks, upside of you position?
- What would you say are the constraints or downsides of your position?
- Would you take this career path again today if given other choices?
- What kind of person would you think is most suitable for this position in terms of personality and skills?

- Is there a more direct path to take to reach this position?
- Can you describe a typical day in your life including the ups and downs of your job?
- What is the most stressful aspect of your position?
- What is the greatest reward you receive from your position?

STEP 2

STEP 2:

Pick a viable industry; interview a key player.

Remember, your job search will not be anything like your parents' job search. As you are well aware, the economy has changed dramatically; technology has evolved in ways that few could have predicted or even imagined. In a sense, you are a twenty-first-century pioneer, preparing to brave the new frontier. Scared? You may be a little—or perhaps even a lot. Excited? You should be. As you make any big transition, you will find that the more information you gather, the better informed your decision and the more satisfied you'll be with the outcomes of your decisions. If you make good decisions the first time around, you will spend less time in life wishing for a time machine and more time just being happy. Therefore we strongly suggest that you take the following steps before you head full-force toward a career.

REVERSE CAREER PATH PLANNING: ONE WAY TO ANSWER THE QUESTION "WHAT DO I WANT TO BE WHEN I GROW UP?"

To children who are certain of their desire to be astronauts, princesses, or fire fighters, this question may seem simple. However, as you get older, you will realize just how complicated the answer to that question can be. One way to begin to address the age-old question is to start where you want to finish. In other words, question someone who has your dream job. You may want to ask him or her: "How did you get to where you are today?" and "Was the journey all that you expected and hoped it would be?" This strategy is often called *reverse career path planning*. The reason this process is considered "reverse" is because you start at the assumed ending point by identifying the position that you eventually hope to land.

"Reversing" the career planning process involves envisioning your desired finish line and, based on that, figuring out how to run the race. This "informational interview" should help you gather information and give you insights into the career you think you want *before* you aggressively pursue that field. You may take this step before you begin undergraduate or graduate school or you may identify a specific job within an industry as you arm yourself for the job hunt.

You must take ownership of this process and be willing to spend the necessary amount of time and energy to gather the information you need. Many business school programs teach this process because it helps students plan their future based on information that can be gathered in the present. This technique can be applied to virtually any industry: from business, legal, and medical fields to engineering, technology, and education. *There is a direct correlation between the amount of information you have and the chances you have of making your plan a reality.*

WHAT'S HOT, WHAT'S NOT, AND WHY SHOULD I CARE?

Even if you think you know exactly the career/position you want, it's wise to consider whether your dream job will be a practical choice in this turbulent economy. Therefore your research into a particular career path should include an investigation into the career's applicability and sustainability. Do you really want to pursue a particular job if no one is hiring for it? Do you want to become an expert in a soon-to-be obsolete area?

You should investigate job areas that are hot right now *and* that show sustainability in the coming decade. For your reading pleasure, we have prepared an overview of just some of these hot career areas that show promise for the coming decade. Some of these areas make our "hot list" because job experts predict increased need in these fields due to anticipated demographic changes or predicted population shifts in the near future. Others are considered "hot" because of the nation's renewed focus on conservation and alternative energy sources or expanding technological advances. New career areas blossom each year. Stay hot on the trail of these new opportunities and pay close attention to your suitability for work in these new and exciting fields.

Many career experts recommend that students watch emerging trends and gather a variety of necessary skills in order to stay hot on the trail of these hot jobs. For example, nurses will need to be experts in electronic records, and marketing students will need to understand social media. As technology jobs grow by the millions, there will be a need for expertise in online security and risk management. The CEO of a top IT research firm suggests that current computer science students couple their studies with courses in marketing, accounting, or finance.

In David Foote's (of Foote Partners) words, "Before, people widely believed that all you needed were deep, nerdy skills...but companies are looking for people with multiple skill sets who can move fluidly with marketing or operations." Researchers are not the only members of the workforce who will need a diverse skill set. The idea of cross training in sports also works in the area of career preparation: the more skills you have to offer, the more marketable you may be. For example, if you're a researcher or analyst, you should try to hone your people skills. If you're in public relations, you may wish to become proficient in computer graphics or data analysis.

Large companies are hiring teams of employees to handle the new emerging social media market. The Bureau of Labor Statistics predicts that such public relations positions should increase 24 percent by 2018. Many universities and community colleges are offering certification programs focusing on Web marketing analytics, Web search optimization, and even user-experience design. Potential employers demanding this expertise range from e-commerce websites to computer game companies. Other new programs combine product design with consumer psychology and behavior.

Jobs in alternative energy fields, such as wind and solar energy, will require engineers to design systems, consultants to monitor usage, and installers and maintainers to manage the systems. Although many finance positions were slashed in the economic crisis, many new jobs have developed in the areas of auditing, compliance, and risk management. Certification in risk management is available through organizations such as the Risk Management Association or the Risk and Insurance Management Society.

In addition, health care continues to see more job openings, with more than four million estimated by 2018. Case managers will be in high demand as well, managing information flow from medical practitioners to insurance companies and hospitals. In the quest to drive down costs, students specializing in nursing informatics will also be in demand. This field requires computer and information sciences to ensure the proper maintenance of patient data.

Next, as you identify new industries that are of interest to you, you may need to do a little more research to better understand job options in these new areas and which careers might best be suited for you. There are several resources that you may wish to consult. Below is a list of the ones we deem to be most useful.

- AIRSdirectory.com – This site provides a list of popular niche job boards. These "niche" job boards are specific to particular career paths and are fertile ground for employers and executive firms.
- Bigtimejobs.com and Nicheboards.com – Similar to above.
- CareerXroads.com – This site lists thousands of websites dedicated to jobs, resumes, and career management.
- The Directory of Employment-Related Internet Sites – Also from Weddle's, this site is very similar but organized by career field.
- The Encyclopedia of Associations – Found in most public libraries, this book contains contact information for groups of individuals in particular fields.
- Indeed.com, Simplyhired.com, and Jobster.com – These job aggregator boards may also provide a lot of helpful information.

- The Million Dollar Directory – Published by Dunn and Bradstreet, this book covers pertinent information about one hundred thousand U.S. corporations.
- The National Trade *and Professional Association Directory* – This directory is another descriptive compendium of organizations.
- Ward's Business Directory – This directory (published by Gale Group) contains data concerning public and private companies.
- The Weddle's Guide to Association Websites – This guide lists associations and employment services for different industry groups.

Keep in mind that once you have located an industry and a company you feel is right for you, there is much to be gained by visiting the specific company's website. In this way, you can obtain even more information about the field or fields that you may wish to pursue.

After you find a potential target area, you should continue the process of *reverse career path planning*. This is a fantastic way to figure out how to get where you want to go. You should contact, and hopefully interview, a person who has your dream job in a "sustainable field." During the interview, you should ask relevant and concise questions to help you figure out if the job in question actually *is* your dream job. If so, it's important to know what you must do to achieve your dream.

At this point, we turn to a more in-depth discussion of each and every step.

TASK ONE: INVESTIGATE *HOT* JOB AREAS

As you are currently uncommitted to a field of study, you have the luxury of being able to see just exactly what's out there. The following "Hot List" was created to help open your mind to the myriad of new opportunities that will be emerging in the new decade. We suggest that you investigate some of these areas as they may give you many new options to pursue in this new and unpredictable economy.

THE HOT LIST FOR THE NEXT DECADE:

You may want to start your investigation with the following career areas. According to *The Occupational Outlook Handbook*, published by the Bureau of Labor Statistics, there are several fields that are projected to grow by more than 21 percent in the coming decade. As hard as this may be to believe, there are also specific job areas that will have more job *openings* than job *seekers*! Not all of the listed careers are projected to have such rapid growth, but there are many other indicators that present a strong case for researching these careers. The Bureau of Labor Statistics predicts that the jobs listed below will be hot through 2018, based on a number of factors, including which sectors of the economy will grow, which sectors will shrink, and what vacancies will evolve as the workforce ages and retires.

HEALTH CARE

Jobs in the health care industry have been some of the most recession-proof in recent history. No matter how much the times change, injured people will always need to be healed and sick people will always need to get well. Potential careers in this field include:

- **Biochemists**
- **Biophysicists**
- **Dental Assistants**
- **Health Information Management Technology**
- **Histotechnology**
- **Home Health Aides**
- **Medical Assistants**
- **Medical Scientists**
- **Mental Health Workers**
- **Nurses**
- **Pharmacy Technicians**
- **Physical Therapist Aides**
- **Physicians' Assistants**
- **Radiology Technicians**
- **Residential Care Workers**
- **Respiratory Therapy**
- **Skin Care Specialists**
- **Speech Language Pathology**
- **Veterinarians**
- **Veterinary Technologists and Technicians**

The aging baby boomers could potentially continue to boost demand for physical therapy and other exercise-science careers, not to mention the need for more health care in general. According to one health care CEO, "The aging of baby boomers is going to drive up demand for all health services, and health care reforms will increase the demand even more." The National Institute of Health reports that nearly 40 million Americans turned 65 or older in 2010. If you have any elderly relatives, you know how much care they can require—imagine helping to take care of 40 million elderly relatives!

In addition to nurses, hospitals will need many other employees in order to deal with this aging population. There will also be an increased need for pharmacists. Also, perhaps not surprisingly, as man needs more health care, so does man's best friend: his pet. According to the American Veterinary Medical Association, *demand will be rising for veterinarians and veterinary technologists as well. The U.S. Labor* Department projects that by 2016, veterinary jobs will increase by 35 percent. Veterinarians will especially be needed to assist those who raise livestock and those who have the responsibility of keeping our food safe.

ENGINEERING

As robotic systems expand, so will the need for *mechanical engineers.* According to Jim Turnquist, director of career services at Michigan Technological University, "In the U.S. we only graduate 70,000 engineers per year, but we're going to need 100,000 per year. The demand is going to go way up." *Civil engineering* and *project engineers* are expected to show an increased demand due to the steady need for private energy and utility projects. Moreover, the recent 2009 stimulus package has set aside ninety billion dollars for public infrastructure. The demand for innovative gadgets and technology will continue to provide many engineering and design opportunities with some of our global computer and electronics companies, such as Intel and Apple. Innovations in the medical community will require skilled engineers. *Domo arrigato, Mr. Roboto!*

SOFTWARE DESIGN AND DEVELOPMENT AND INFORMATION TECHNOLOGIES

As our society becomes more tech-savvy—and therefore tech-dependent—*all* industries will need more of the following:

- **Information Technology (IT) Experts**
- **Networking Specialists**
- **Programmers**
- **Proprietary Application Designers**
- **Software Engineers**
- **Troubleshooters**
- **Web Design Specialists**

Most businesses today depend upon the stability of their computer networks. Analysts show that IT experts will continue to be in demand for quite some time. Job openings in services related to computer system design are also expected to grow nearly 40 percent as more businesses begin to rely on the latest and greatest technologies.

EDUCATION

Why is there such a high demand for qualified teachers? If you are thinking about going into teaching, you might be comforted by the findings of the National Center for Education Statistics, which say that in the coming eight years, demand will grow for 2.8 million *additional* teachers. This increase is due to retirements, higher student demand, mandatory enforcement of smaller classroom sizes, and teacher turnover.

Some areas in the country will have a much greater demand for teachers than others. It is important to do your research about where you wish to live and how many openings in the field of education there are each year in that area. On February 2, 2010, the *Wall Street Journal* reported that spending on education will expand by nine percent by 2011. This increase in spending is a part of the federal government's plan to advance its overhaul of federal school funding policy. Speaking of budget...

AUDITING AND FACTORING

Whether auditors work for accounting firms or as internal auditors for businesses, there is a growing demand for members of the profession. For one, the billions of dollars of stimulus money must be tracked. Additionally, businesses are under more scrutiny than ever before. In a way, auditors are comparable to detectives who are armed with calculators.

With commercial loans becoming increasingly difficult to obtain, factoring allows small businesses to obtain funding based on their accounts receivable, also known as the money that the businesses expect to collect. *Factors* are skilled experts in calculating and interpreting these amounts. With no end to the financial rollercoaster in sight, factoring jobs will most likely continue to thrive.

GREEN CAREERS

It seems as though a certain "inconvenient truth" has finally become convenient. Sometimes called *green-collar jobs*, these environmentally conscious occupations appear to be here to stay—for a while at least. Some of these opportunities include:

- **"Green" Auditors**
- **"Green" Designers**
- **"Green" Technicians**
- **Water and Waste Management Analysts and Operators**

In many ways, these green-collar jobs are just blue-collar jobs that have a better respect for the environment. For example, a steel worker is a green-collar worker if he or she is working on a solar energy project. The 2009 stimulus package includes funds for investment in new green programs, which creates potential for new jobs. Some of these new jobs may include:

- **Civil Engineers**
- **Environmental Compliance Specialists**
- **Nuclear Operations Engineers**
- **Recycling Center Operations**
- **Solar Operations Engineers**
- **Urban Planners**
- **Waste Water Engineers**
- **Water Quality Consultants**
- **Wind Operations Engineers**

ENERGY

As the national government increases spending on renewable energy, the number of jobs available in this area will increase as well. Specifically, exciting new jobs will surface in the industries of *nuclear, wind, and solar power.* Nuclear energy appears to be a growth industry, with as many as twenty-six new nuclear power plants being proposed for just the next decade alone. The use of wind and solar energy has been increasing across the country as well.

BIOTECHNOLOGY AND BIOSCIENCE

One of the decade's most exciting growth areas, biotechnology, refers to the use of organisms, cells, or biomolecules to solve problems in our society or to create new products. *Bioscience* is the broader term referring to biology-related industries such as medical devices and diagnostics. Many new drugs are developed through bioscience. In addition, bioscience is also helping to develop technology, such as in obtaining and analyzing DNA evidence and using this evidence in criminal cases. If you're a *Law and Order* fan, this field might just be for you. Many people with aptitudes in science or math might also find this new career a good match.

Some positions in bioscience are available after a two-year degree program, and many of these degree programs are offered at many schools. Often academics are paired with internships. Positions available in this area include:
- **Laboratory Management**
- **Laboratory Technicians**
- **Quality Assurance Specialists**

- **Research Scientists**
- **Sales Representatives**

Some companies and research institutes also provide employees with tuition reimbursements. Many biotech jobs offer positions to individuals who have a two-year degree and allow them to pursue their four-year degree while working in the field. Bioscience fields are targeted as high-growth areas as the economy retools.

THE ENTREPRENEURIAL OPTION

Some industrious young graduates may want to launch their own companies. Becoming your own boss may prove to be an exciting and lucrative career path, especially when jobs are scarce. The largest hurdle for most entrepreneurs is finding the funding to start up the enterprise. Lemonade stands and bake sales will not raise enough. Since start-up cash may be difficult to come by, it becomes very important to tap into the resources of your network. Try to contact established businesspeople and other alumni of the schools you attended. Some investors will offer seed money in exchange for a stake in the business.

A recent report from the *Wall Street Journal* profiles several innovative and hard-working entrepreneurs who have been able to turn small business ventures into profitable businesses. The common denominator driving these self-starters appears to be having the commitment, energy, and resilience to put in the thousands of hours required to reach success. Moreover, these frugal pioneers utilized technological tools such as professional-looking websites and automated phone-answering systems to make their fledgling companies more attractive to potential customers.

Traditionally, start-ups have proved to be dauntingly expensive. One study from Babson College estimates that an average start-up can run $65,000 for inventory, equipment, and payroll. According to the Kauffman Foundation, a nonprofit organization devoted to entrepreneurship, the cost for a start-up can go even higher. For example, a retail start-up may start around $98,000 while a manufacturing start-up, $175,000. Although many start-ups fail due to a lack of capital, start-up costs have plummeted in the last decade. According to Bo Fishback, vice president of entrepreneurship of the Kauffman Foundation, "It's gotten so much easier to reach mass markets and test out ideas. This is something that's becoming accessible to anyone with an idea."

On the positive side, most young entrepreneurs are well suited for the hard work and long hours that the launching of a company demands. Many members of your generation are technologically savvy, with great skills in social networking. These two attributes are both very helpful when publicizing a new product or service. In this respect, you have an advantage over your well-seasoned and more conservative counterparts. Many schools' campuses have competitions to help fund and actualize company start-ups. For example, Babson College—ranked the best among all colleges in entrepreneurship—hosts an annual Entrepreneurship Forum and supports winning business plans with funds, consulting, and other valuable services. The University of Miami's Launch Pad program, offered by the campus career center, helps support the creation of business plans and offers additional guidance. Several independent training programs have begun to pop up all over the country, including "boot camps" such as TechStars in Boulder, Colorado, and Y Combinator in Mountain View, California. These groups offer advice on planning, marketing, and other networking opportunities.

OTHER HOT AREAS:

The areas of *national security* and *international affairs* are producing many new jobs as well. The Bureau of Labor Statistics predicts that job growth is expected within the Department of Homeland Security and other agencies due to an increased number of retiring workers. There are also proposals in the 2011 budget for a 2.1 percent increase in defense spending, which would bring the budget from $693.5 billion to $708 billion.

If you're considering a career in journalism, you should keep an eye on the *Internet publishing and broadcasting field*, which is also a burgeoning area. As print journalism steadily declines, news, information, and entertainment will be spread more exclusively through new media technologies.

Workers in the *human resources industry* will also continue to be in high demand. The Bureau of Labor Statistics predicts that the industry will grow faster than average in the next decade. Additionally, the *social assistance industry* is projected to grow, leading to jobs ranging from *family counselors* to *social workers* and *program administrators*.

TASK TWO: FIGURING OUT WHAT WORK WORKS FOR YOU

What Questions Must I Ask Myself?

Congratulations! Now that you have a sense for the industries that are growing, you'll be able to complete the next step: identifying the one that most intrigues you. What job can you see yourself holding that would genuinely make you happy? Don't consider who you think you're *supposed* to be; that person will never be as happy as the you who follows your heart. You must determine what is important for you to know about your prospective career choice. The questions below are only valuable if *You* are the one answering them—not your parents, teachers, peers, or significant other. Your parents might want you to carry on the family tradition of practicing criminal law while your favorite art teacher thinks you have an incredible aptitude for making pottery. However, there are no "shoulds." Of course those closest to you will be able to provide great feedback if you're struggling to find answers. Yet the process must begin with *you*.

As a start:

- What truly excites/interests me?
- What kinds of people are attracted to this field? Would I want to befriend these people or under different circumstances would I have nothing to do with them?
- How much education is necessary or advisable for this position?
- How much money am I willing to invest in my future to land this position?

- Is there upward mobility? How much responsibility do I ultimately wish to have?
- Will I be able to have a rich family life and to spend time with my family if a family is something I want?
- Would it be possible for me to step away from the position for a while and re-enter later if I felt it was necessary?
- Will it be better for me to live in a particular location to maximize my options?
- Does the particular practice of this job vary from location to location?

Finding the answers to these questions will help you to determine whether you are making the right decision *the first time around.* It's important to know in advance whether you're heading down the best career path for *you.* However, this significant juncture in your life should not be filled with anxiety or worry. Instead, take some adventurous, enlightening steps toward gathering the kind of information you'll need in order to begin heading in the right direction.

TASK THREE: USING THE PROCESS TO FIGURE OUT HOW TO GET TO YOUR DREAM CAREER

The purpose of the above-mentioned process is to understand not only what you're getting yourself into, but also the best way to arrive at your chosen destination. The idea is to discover *how* a person who has reached your chosen destination got there. It's also important to know what mentors this person may have had along the way, and which steps were critical in terms of education and experience. Moreover, ask the person whom you choose to interview exactly what has *not* worked along the way. Did he or she experience any pitfalls that could have been avoided?

HOW DO I FIND THIS CONTACT PERSON?

Unfortunately, role models do not grow on trees (it would look rather odd if they did). You will have to take the initiative in tracking down a person who has the job you desire. The references section of this book contain the names of several associations that will help get you on the right track. Parents and their network of friends and associates may also help you find this contact. If a face-to-face meeting is not possible, then contact this person by phone or e-mail. However, keep in mind that the more personal the interview, the better the information. Sometimes an administrative assistant will be designated to help answer your questions. Treat this person with as much respect as you would give to his or her boss.

WHAT SHOULD I SAY TO GET THE INTERVIEW?

Be brief, polite, and clear that your intention is to gather information. The key is in your approach: ask for a few minutes of time, not a job, and most people will be happy to help you. Once you have made contact, ask for referrals to other people who may be able to help you. Remember, these wise and worldly individuals have been in your shoes and thus can relate to you. As them the following questions:

- How did you land in the city where you live? Do you like where you are? Do you intend to stay?
- Do you have any advice for others who wish to do what you do? Do you have any regrets? Did you se-

lect the right career for yourself? What suggestions would you have for a young person who aspires to someday hold a position like yours?

- Do you intend to stay in this job or is it a stepping stone for a future job? Do you intend to get more education?
- Do you anticipate "opting out" to raise a family or do you have a plan in place? Does your current position allow flextime options?
- What are your daily responsibilities? Can you describe "a day in the life" of your job?
- What are the best perks of your job? What are your main challenges and stressors?
- What makes your job difficult (i.e. long hours, nights, travel, work environment, lack of support staff, etc.)?
- Are you happy with your career choice? Why or why not?
- Would you consider this job again if you were entering the market today? Why or why not?
- How would you describe your job?

CHAPTER TO-DO LIST:

- Plan ahead. Remember, it's all about envisioning where you want to be in five or maybe ten years. A little planning now, as you choose a career, will greatly pay off as you begin your adult life.
- Take the time to ask yourself the questions posed earlier in the chapter. This will help you figure out where you hope to go in life.
- Now that you have a sense for the industries that are growing, identify the one that most intrigues you.

If you can't see yourself following one of the paths mentioned in the chapter, don't fret. There are many other viable careers out there.

- Begin to explore the "who's who" in the industry of your choice.
- Try to identify a specific person in one of the firms who holds the position you find most desirable. This is ultimately the person you will want to set up an informational interview with in order to discover more about how he or she rose to that place in his or her career. Discovering the daily responsibilities that come with the job is also crucial.
- Remember: The goal of this process is to learn as much as you possibly can about the person whom you choose to interview. Try to establish the daily ups and downs of his or her career in order to assess if this is truly a career you want to pursue. If your gut tells you that this person is under excessive stress and mainlining coffee in order to stay alive, you may want to take that into account and consider a different and more fulfilling path.

CHAPTER TO-DON'T LIST:

- Do not make rash decisions. This is your life; don't rush into it.
- Do not allow your loved ones to convince you to follow a path that you haven't chosen. You will never be able to give yourself to your profession unless you are passionate about it.
- Do not be pushy during your informational interview. Remember, this person has generously given you

his or her time to help you understand the facts of the profession you are hoping to follow *not* to interview you for a potential job opening. However, you should always carry your resume with you in case someone asks to see it.

- Do not allow yourself to be consumed by stress. If you ever feel yourself becoming overwhelmed, do something that you find pleasurable and relaxing, i.e. taking a walk, meeting a friend, working out, etc. In other words, pick a healthy way to refresh yourself.

STEP 3

STEP 3:

Select a thriving place that offers your chosen industry.

It is no secret that today's economy is both volatile and unpredictable. However, this unfortunate truth should not induce a panic attack. Regardless of the daunting reports on twenty-four-hour news networks, the search for a meaningful career doesn't have to be as frightening or as stressful as you think. That being said, it is now more important than ever to develop a sensible path to select a career *area*. With the rapid pace of economic change, it's wise to investigate cities with sustainability. You have spent far too much time selecting the perfect location to attend university to not put thought into your postgraduate home. Use the same energy and enthusiasm you had during your college search to get excited about where your career might take you.

Finding a job in the place you grew up may not be easy in a difficult economy. You may never have considered looking elsewhere—but we urge you to do so. Consider the kind of lifestyle that you wish to lead and what you need to be happy. Then do some research on different locations in this diverse country and at least ponder the question of where you may find a satisfying career as well as a wonderful lifestyle well suited to your personality and values. Here are some relevant questions that will help you start this process:

- Do I want to walk or drive to work?
- Do I want to be able to take interesting road trips on the weekends?
- Do I want to live in an urban area?
- Do I mind a commute and/or traffic?

Answering these questions will help you begin to identify what's important to you in terms of day-to-day living. Additionally, if a harsh economy forces you to lose your job, it would be beneficial to be in a city that will present you with more opportunities to get your life back on track. Common sense should tell you that if you live in a place with thriving industries that need people who do what you do, your chances of finding a new position are favorable. For example, if you're a labor lawyer and live in a city with not only a glut of lawyers but also a diminishing number of large businesses, then you may have a great deal of difficulty finding a new job if you're let go. The bottom line: if you're planning to start your life, plan to be in a place that will help you have a long career!

HOME IS WHERE THE HEART IS:

There are some situations in which staying in your hometown may provide excellent circumstances for you to start your career. This is because many fortunate individuals have families that are both supportive and well connected. If this is true for you, then perhaps you may want to consider returning home after college or graduate school. Family connections are an excellent source of networking. Your family members may be able to open doors for you that you may have difficulty opening on your own. However, in this economy, whether you're hired or not will likely be determined by your potential, not your connections. So getting the job is still up to you. Family connections may also help you if you venture to a new city by opening doors for interviews and further networking. Moreover, a supportive family can ease the transition as you move to a new city. Don't underestimate the challenge of moving to a completely new venue without having any support network.

Thus, the idea of a "home base" is also one to consider if you decide to look elsewhere to begin your adult life. Ask yourself these questions to help you investigate this issue:

- Is the city I'm choosing to live in a great place for ME to establish a new home base?
- Is this new community one where my family could grow?
- Can I see myself providing the new family stronghold?
- Would my parents ever considering moving to where I am (if that is something I want)?

While you may not be able to see far into the future where your parents are shuffling around the house in slippers and you're bouncing a horde of grandchildren on your knee, envisioning the kind of family life you could have in your new home is still helpful and necessary.

YOUR ROAD MAP TO SUCCESS:

The following city guide provides you with a *model* for your personal research. We are not trying to push you toward certain cities or a particular field. The cities that we present to you here made the cut as a result of extensive research regarding their potential for sustainability in the near future. Despite the fact that we have created this list for you, you should still do your own research to investigate different parts of the country and the opportunities that are available in each region.

This exercise is meant to reduce any anxiety you may feel when it comes to selecting a viable career path. By following this structure, you can feel safer knowing that you are approaching these tough economic times with a systematic, organized approach. If jobs are scarce in the area you're considering, don't be afraid to look elsewhere. Find a place where your industry is growing. If you perform this research now, you will most likely prevent yourself from making a poor and costly decision later. Remember: plan now, payoff later.

You should also keep in mind the fact that you have the advantage of youth on your side, meaning that you don't have as much to risk in making a big career change or moving to a new city. As you get older and settle down, your investment in the place that you live grows, as does your risk of change. *Be willing to take chances now, while you're young, so that you don't miss out on any opportunities for a better life.* By having an idea of where you plan to be in ten or fifteen years, and whether that city will suit your long-term needs, you are using your practical intelligence to think ahead. This sort of sophisticated mindset will give you the competitive edge needed in the business world as well.

As you know, one of the biggest risks a person can take is deciding to move to a new city. However, this risk is often well worth taking, as long as you take the time to consider everything that moving entails. Be sure to ask yourself: Where do I ultimately want to settle? Close family and friends can contribute to your decision (in a positive or negative way). Many parents have the attitude that their children should settle where their roots are: near them, and oftentimes, as we previously mentioned, moving back to the place you grew up can make sense. However, you should try to be open to all opportunities—whether they are in your hometown, in state, or across the country. Go to where the best opportunities are. Then, using that practical intelligence we keep mentioning, try to imagine whether or not you would be happy and successful in that place. You shouldn't have to give up your family for your career or your career for your family if you don't want to.

The rest of this chapter provides you with some city characterizations to serve as models for the research you should do as you consider possible places to live. Again remember that this list does not contain *every* city in the country that is thriving economically. It should be used as a guide more than anything else. As our favorite doctor once wrote, "Oh the places you'll go!"

PLACES TO GO, PLACES TO SEE:

It is important to realize that where you live will determine the scope of opportunities that will become available to you in your career. You should always hope for the best but be prepared for the worst. If the job you are initially hired for doesn't work out, it will be to your advantage to have settled in a city where there are many thriving industries. Richard Florida, a prominent professor of business and creativity at the Rotman School of Management (University of Toronto), offers academic research that supports our recommendations to research *where* you may wish to settle. In fact, he suggests that *the decision of where to live is the single most important decision you will make in your life*. According to Florida in his book *Who's Your City? How the Creative Economy is Making Where to Live the Most Important Decision of Your Life*, this choice is more influential than career or relationship choices. Other influential factors include: the impacts of the type of jobs you will have access to, your social network, your family and lifestyle choices, and your potential wealth and overall happiness. In his book, Florida ranks every city in the United States—in detail—including the best places for recent college graduates, young professionals, and young families. The award-winning author also suggests using an online "PlaceFinder" tool to help you find the best fit. The PlaceFinder website programs are designed to generate potential homes from user data and then creating a virtual tour via Google Earth.

Florida argues that the most creative people tend to select cities that offer the stimulation of other creative people. This clustering then begins to foster technological progress and economic growth. Moving is very common in this country, with approximately forty million Americans moving each year! This trend will likely continue as more and more young adults choose to leave home and move to a city that suits a particular work interest and lifestyle.

READY, SET, GO!

Buckle up your seat belt, because we are going to take you on a ride around the United States to see some of the most prosperous large cities and what they have to offer. All you need is an open mind and a little bit of enthusiasm. The cities listed below are not the *only* places that are prospering in these troubled economic times; they are merely the cities that *we* found to be exceptional. For each city, we provide a summary of important information as well as a breakdown of cost of living, taxes, economy, population, and major businesses. These are some of the factors you should take into consideration as you investigate how livable a given city may be for you. Following each city description, you will find an eclectic list of companies that you may wish to investigate for job opportunities. While this list is not intended to be exhaustive, it is a starting point to see the diversity of opportunity that may be available.

We have listed each city with the most current Consumer Price Index available at the time of printing. The CPI is calculated by observing price changes among a wide array of products in urban areas and weighing these price changes by the share of income consumers spend purchasing them. The resulting statistic is a very popular measure of gauging the cost of living in a particular place.

WHY ATLANTA?

Population: 537,000 in the city (5.3 million in the greater metro area)

Cost of living index: 97.6 (national average is 100)

Atlanta, Georgia, not only offers a great climate and plenty of opportunities to show team spirit at Braves baseball games, it's also a very business-friendly city. Metropolitan Atlanta was ranked among the "Top 25" on *Forbes'* 2009 list of "Best Places for Business and Careers." The region is growing, business is thriving, and the nightlife is hopping. Because Atlanta is pro-business in its tax structure, large corporations such as The Home Depot, CNN, and Coca-Cola find it advantageous to locate there.

Impressively, Atlanta is home to nine companies on the 2009 Fortune 500 list. It is also one of the country's leading cities in high-tech employment, ranking high in telecommunication services employment, as well as software publishing and IT service jobs. Atlanta also houses many world-class universities and hospitals.

BUSINESSES TO INVESTIGATE:

- **AFLAC Insurance**

- **Asbury Automotive Group**

- **CIBA Vision**

- **CNN**

- **Coca-Cola**

- **Delta Airlines**

- **Genuine Parts Co.**

- **Gulfstream Aerospace**

- **The Home Depot**

- **Newell Rubbermaid**

- **Southern Co.**

- **SunTrust Banks**

- **United Parcel Service**

WHY AUSTIN?

Population: 757,000 in the city (1.5 million in the greater metro area)

Cost of Living Index: 94

Many consider Austin to be a creative-class capital, with a well-educated population and a high percentage of young residents fueling the metro area. The youthful population also gives the city a vibrant nightlife. If you like to dance, you will feel well at home in this musical city with its high number of live music venues. Equally as exciting is the fact that Austin is also one of the top cities in the country in terms of business start-ups per capita.

Forbes magazine (one of our favorites, in case you hadn't noticed) rates Austin as one of "America's Best Value Cities," based on its low inflation rate, growth projections, and a respectable median cost of living. This speaks to the strength of the city's energy and technology sectors, which are what most economists look at in order to determine future growth.

As a state, Texas has a global manufacturing sector, which is no small feat in this day and age. Moreover Texas boasts the lowest workers' compensation costs of any state and also lacks an income or capital gains tax for its citizens.

BUSINESSES TO INVESTIGATE:

- **Advanced Micro Devices**
- **AT&T**
- **City of Austin**

- **Dell Computer Inc.**

- **Freescale Semiconductors**

- **IBM Corporation**

- **Seton Healthcare Network**

- **Solectron Texas**

- **St. David's Healthcare**

- **The State of Texas**

- **University of Texas**

WHY BALTIMORE?

Population: 637,000 in the city (2.6 million in the greater metro area)

Cost of Living Index: 121

Baltimore's strategic location as an east coast port central to many major East Coast cities continues to make it attractive to new and expanding businesses. It exports coal, grain, iron, steel, and copper, and remains a center for shipbuilding. Service sector fields such as law, finance, medicine, hospitality, maritime commerce, and health are in abundance. Teachers specializing in primary and secondary education are in high demand in Baltimore City and in the Baltimore County Public Schools. The high-tech market is also growing in areas such as electronics, IT services, telecommunications, aerospace research, and video game design.

The home of the Baltimore Ravens is known for more than Michael Phelps and Edgar Allen Poe. It's also the national headquarters for advanced medical research and treatment and home to top teaching hospitals such as Johns Hopkins and the University Hospital at the University of Maryland. Moreover, Baltimore is a research center for human genome mapping.

Don't be misled: Baltimore living is not all work and no play. The Inner Harbor renovation has made it the place to be in Maryland, with shopping, dining, and an amazing aquarium. The Inner Harbor renovation has brought great change to Baltimore: an increase in the number of urban dwellers and more tourism to the city.

BUSINESSES TO INVESTIGATE:

- **Black & Decker**

- **Constellation Energy**

- **U.S. Foodservice**

WHY BOSTON?

Population: 609,000 in the city (4.4 million in the greater metro area)

Cost of Living Index: 129

Although Boston has a higher cost of living than many other parts of the country, it boasts a powerful mutual fund industry, a dynamic high-tech sector, and a *brain trust* of many of the country's top colleges, universities, hospitals, and research institutions. Harvard University, MIT, Boston

College, Boston University, and Brandeis University are a few of the top schools in or immediately outside of metropolitan Boston. These esteemed schools attract companies that wish to take advantage of the intellectual and creative capital being cultivated in these schools. These institutions hire thousands of Boston residents, since the city has a high number of skilled workers and a strong international reputation. Beantown is also a cultural center for creative talent. It still has the same colonial charm it always had. The city has a lot to offer in terms of culture and entertainment from museums, to duck tours, to whale watching.

Boston is emerging with a new convention center and a new waterfront development plan. Continuing development is a good thing to look for when researching a city. Boston also happens to be a in a prime location with great access to the entire East Coast.

BUSINESSES TO INVESTIGATE:

- **Akamai Technologies**

- **Beacon Roofing Supply**

- **Biogen Idec**

- **Boston Consulting Group**

- **Bruker Corp**

- **Cubist Pharmaceuticals**

- **NetScout Systems**

- **Parexel International Corp.**

- **Pegasystems**

- **Sapient Corp.**

- **Senior Housing Properties Trust**

- **Sepracor**

- **Starent Networks Corp.**

- **State Street Corp.**

- **Thermo Fisher Scientific**

- **TJX Cos.**

- **VistaPrint Ltd.**

- **Zoll Medical Corp.**

WHY CHICAGO?

Population: 2.8 million in the city (9.4 million in the greater metro area)

Cost of Living Index: 133

Chicago offers a strategic location, a diverse workforce, and many world-class schools, such as Northwestern University and the University of Chicago, and a strong economic infrastructure, strengthened by companies that represent virtually every sector of our national economy. Chicago is a business capital, home to several world-leading economic exchanges. In addition to having a thriving workplace, Chicago is also a hub for cultural activities. Chicago hosts amazing museums, Broadway shows, an orchestra, dance troupes, opera, and so much more. Described as a very livable city, Chicago features thriving downtown living areas and easy access from nearby suburbs.

In order to keep the infrastructure strong, Chicago invests nearly a billion dollars annually in schools, roads, parks, public transportation, and airports. It is no wonder that Chicago alone takes care of one-third of all nonstop flights to China. Known as the "data recovery capital of North America," Chicago has a digital infrastructure that allows for real-time exchanges with Europe and Asia. Chicago Public Schools even offer the largest Chinese language program in the country.

The downtown lifestyle is booming and exciting with dozens of cultural institutions, major league sports, and a beautiful lakefront. The lakefront alone has enough to keep you busy, with special events, walking, jogging, cycling, a beach area, and even chess tables. The *New York Times* calls Chicago "the quintessential American city." Check mate!

Chi-town is eco-friendly as well. Chicago has created or planned more than two million square feet of green roofs and recently planned new green spaces, planting over half a million trees. Even though there are millions of people in the city, there is plenty of oxygen to go around!

The Chicago Sustainable Business Alliance is a network dedicated to assisting enterprises hoping to incorporate sustainability into their practices and products. The alliance provides connections, resources, and help for these companies. Many large companies, such as Boeing, have moved their corporate headquarters to the Chicago arena.

BUSINESSES TO INVESTIGATE:

- **Accenture**

- **Assurance Agency Ltd.**

- **Boeing**

- **CareerBuilder**

- **Caterpillar**

- **Digitas**

- **Google Inc.**

- **McKinsey & Company**

- **Microsoft**

- **Northwestern Mutual Financial Network**

- **Paychex**

- **Resources Global Professionals**

- **Transwestern Commercial Services**

- **Whole Foods**

WHY HOUSTON?

Population: 2.2 million in the city (5.4 million in the greater metro area)

Cost of Living Index: 89

Houston, as you can see from the above calculations, is a city filled to the brim with people. Rather than hinder the city, its enormous population helps it to win many awards such as "Top Metro in the Nation" (*Site Selection Magazine*, March 2009) and second "Best City for Jobs" (*Forbes*, April 2009).

Downtown Houston is proud of its multibillion-dollar expansion of its medical center, which has stimulated a stream of high-earning workers looking to live in the area. Also, at this point, Houston has no formal zoning code. Thus, in Houston, old homes may be torn down and rebuilt without a great deal of red tape. Like all of the cities on our list, Houston does not have a shortage of employment. The oil companies continue to bring jobs to the city, as the energy business is the cornerstone of Houston's economy. It is close to many refineries and offers excellent travel options.

Houston is also home to 26 Fortune 500 companies and has 23 active foreign chambers of commerce and trade associations. In addition, eleven foreign banks operate there. You can practically travel around the world without ever leaving Houston.

The health care industry is thriving as well, with the Texas Medical Center treating over five million patients each year. A joint venture between the University of Texas M.D. Anderson and the UT Health Science Center is focused on biotechnology and life sciences research. The Baylor College of Medicine is home to the Human Genome Sequencing Center—one of only five in the entire country. Houston is also a center for the technology industry, with over one thousand computer-related companies and the

Houston Technology Center, which has boosted technology entrepreneurship and helped more than 150 emerging companies.

BUSINESSES TO INVESTIGATE:

- **Amerada Hess**

- **AT&T**

- **Chevron**

- **Citgo Energy**

- **Conoco Phillips**

- **Global Santa Fe**

- **Lockheed Martin**

- **Phillips**

WHY MINNEAPOLIS/ST. PAUL?

Population: 390,000 in the city (3.1 million in the greater metro area)

Cost of Living Index: 114

The twin cities of Minneapolis and St. Paul (MSP) are heralded for a wide variety of cultural attractions, including several fine museums, such as the Walker Art Center and the Minneapolis Sculpture Garden, as well as the Science Museum of Minnesota. The St. Anthony Main District, located along the Mississippi River and just west of downtown, is the oldest area of Minneapolis. The Guthrie Theater, Minneapolis's premiere theater venue, contains three theaters, including the one that was used for years when Guthrie was located in the Walker Art Center.

Minneapolis is an industrial and commercial center, home to 15 Fortune 500 companies, 30 Fortune 1000 companies, and the Ninth Federal Reserve Bank. It is also listed on the *Forbes* 2009 "Best Places for Business and Careers." Metro MSP is also ranked as the second best U.S. city in which to make a living.

In another survey, *Forbes* ranked the metro area very highly in terms of housing, affordability, inflation, fuel economy, and potential job growth. MSP is a big area for manufacturing electronics, machinery, medical products, food processing, and graphic arts. Thus it produces a wide variety of useful items. The city also hosts one of the largest concentrations of high-tech firms in the nation, which are supported by the many scientists and engineers who graduate from the University of Minnesota and other nearby colleges. MSP also has programs that provide finance packages for businesses expanding or relocating to the cities. These programs have been very successful.

The twin cities are also considered to be one of the largest trucking hubs in the country. This important economic factor is evident in the overall freight capacity of the cargo service carriers at the MSP International Airport, the four railroad companies' network, and the 150 motor freight companies that operate in the area. The airport alone sees more than 170,000 tons of freight each year. Much of this freight is imported and exported to and from local and foreign markets.

The region has also been distinguished by awards such as the "Healthiest Hearts in the Nation" award, which proves that the cities' populations are very healthy. MSP has also done a lot to reduce pollution, which contributes to the health of its citizens. These cities are also a great place to be single! *Forbes* has put them in their top ten lists of "Best Cities for Singles."

BUSINESSES TO INVESTIGATE:

- **Allina Health**

- **Fairview Health Services**

- **Mayo Clinic**

- **Northwest Airlines**

- **State of Minnesota**

- **Target**

- **University of Minnesota**

- **Wells Fargo**

- **3M**

WHY PHOENIX?

Population: 1.6 million in the city (4.2 million in the greater metro area)

Cost of Living Index: 100

Phoenix boasts a wealth of programs to support large and small business. These programs do everything from helping businesses to gain grants and funding opportunities to making it easier to gain zoning and permits. The region also possesses a growing and skilled workforce. Many Phoenix-based companies have been recognized for their efforts to create high-quality working environments, which is very important and difficult to find due to the decline of unions. The economic base of Phoenix rests partially on advanced technology, aerospace, and service industries. As you can see, the temperature is not the only thing that is *hot, hot, hot.*

Phoenix is one of the fastest growing, multicultural cities in the country and has shown a historical commitment to business diversity. The city strives to advance the economic growth of local businesses through its Minority, Woman and Small Business Enterprise (MWSBE) Program. Through a coordinated effort among several city departments, the MWSBE Program provides MWSBE certification, procurement opportunities, construction subcontracting utilization, small business management, technical assistance, and educational services and networking opportunities.

BUSINESSES TO INVESTIGATE:

- **American Express Co.**

- **Banner Health**

- **Cox Communications**

- **Deloitte & Touche**

- **Dial Corp.**

- **Edward Jones**

- **Henry & Horne PLC**

- **Honeywell**

- **Intel Corp.**

- **McMurray**

- **Medtronic Microelectronics Center**

- **MFS Investment Management Regional Office**

- **Ritz-Carlton Hotel Co.**

- **State Mortgage LLC**

- **Target**

- **Troon Golf**

- **USAA**

- **Wells Fargo**

WHY PITTSBURGH?

Population: 312,000 in the city (2.3 million in the greater metro area)

Cost of Living Index: 92

Pittsburgh has weathered the early twenty-first century recession far better than most cities. The Pittsburgh area is now home to eight Fortune 500 companies and thirteen Fortune 1000 headquarters. The city also boasts Global Links, a redirector of medical supplies worldwide.

Despite the city's reputation, it has managed to go from gray to green. Pittsburgh has undergone a dramatic environmental transformation, and its streets are now home to trees planted by the city. It stands out as a leader with more green square footage than any other large U.S. city. The David L. Lawrence Convention Center is the world's first certified green convention center, and it has set the bar for the greening of other public buildings nationwide, with annual energy savings of over 30 percent.

The downtown area is easy to traverse by foot, and it hosts a children's museum, the Heinz History Center—a Smithsonian affiliate—the Phipps Conservatory, Botanical Gardens, and the Pittsburgh Glass Center. From this information, we can conclude that you will never have a dull weekend in Pittsburgh.

In addition to many tourist attractions, there are many riverfront trails and places to kayak. Biking is also a great hobby in Pittsburgh. According to *BIKE* magazine, Pittsburgh has earned a ranking in the top five cities for mountain biking. Biking is also a great means of transportation, with over one hundred public art bike racks installed. For longer trips, there is an excellent public transportation system and a free downtown "T" subway.

The colleges in the Pittsburgh area include Carnegie Mellon, University of Pittsburgh, Duquesne, and Slippery Rock. The city has invested in hybrid vehicles and also plans to turn the waste form Heinz Field into bio-diesel fuel. You might be interested to know that the city has one community garden for every 3,000 residents, almost 200 citywide.

BUSINESSES TO INVESTIGATE:

- **Heinz**

- **PNC**

- **PPG Industries**

- **U.S. Steel**

WHY RALEIGH/DURHAM?

Population: 392,000 in the city (1 million in the greater metro area)

Cost of Living Index: 100

While the major U.S. labor markets were reporting job losses, Raleigh and Durham, North Carolina, still managed to rank high among metro areas in terms of job retention. Raleigh and Durham have seen tremendous population growth in the past decade as well. These twin cities of the South offer wonderful weather, prestigious universities, excellent hospitals, and a plethora of emerging businesses.

The two cities often grab the country's attention because of their highly educated workforce, low business costs, and projected job growth. Within this region, the Research Triangle Park area is home to 170 companies employing over 42,000 people. The North Carolina market emerges as a leader in small business activity.

In one recent report, Durham was listed as having one of the highest percentages of workers labeled "creative class." Raleigh cracks the top ten as the best city for jobs overall. The area is ranked by *Forbes* as the "#1 City Where People are Relocating" for 2009. *Forbes* also named Durham as the third best place for business and careers in 2009. *Fortune Small Business* gave Durham high marks as one of the "Best Place[s] to Live and Launch," and the *Sporting News* ranks the area as one of the Best Sports Cities in the United States.

BUSINESSES TO INVESTIGATE:

- **Biogen Idec**

- **Cisco Systems**

- **IBM**

WHY SEATTLE?

Population: 598,000 in the city (3.3 million in the greater metro area)

Cost of living index: 114

It may never have occurred to you that Seattle can offer you a great deal more than just a good cup of java. This socially conscious and creative city has initiated many programs to improve neighborhoods and inject new life into the small business community. Seattle also offers a healthy blend of small businesses and a large concentration of manufacturing industries in aircraft, transportation equipment, and forest products, which perhaps contributes to its success in international trade. It's also a hub for advanced technology in computer software, electronics, biotechnology, medical equipment, and environmental engineering.seattle's manufacturing industry is highly productive, offering high wages and job security in this tech-intensive city. Because of its tech-intensive economy, Seattle's manufacturing industry is still very productive, offering high wages and an impressive amount of job security. The state also has very low taxes. Washington doesn't have its own income tax or capital gains tax; this makes it easier for small businesses to thrive.

Minimal taxation is not the only way in which Seattle takes care of its residents. It is proactive in responding to travel congestion problems caused by urban sprawl. The local government also has programs to provide efficient public transportation and affordable public housing. The city has also set forth the Seattle Climate Action Plan, a $37 million package to fund initiatives to help people conserve fuel in cars, homes, and the workplace.

Seattle is a mecca for the aerospace industry with several companies, such as Boeing, having a strong local presence. Typically, the term "aerospace" is used to refer to the industry that researches, designs, manufactures, operates, and maintains vehicles moving through air and space.

Aerospace is a diverse field, with a multitude of commercial, industrial, and military applications. Commercial shipping is also a thriving industry in Seattle, as the Port of Seattle is the fifth largest container port in the United States.

As if these economic and political reasons were not enough to convince you to pack your bags right now, some of the largest health magazines (such as *Men's Health* and *Women's Health*) have ranked it as one of America's healthiest cities. Seattle is ranked as the fourth healthiest city for men and the third healthiest city for women. If a family is something you someday hope to have, such a healthy and vibrant city could be an excellent place to start one.

BUSINESSES TO INVESTIGATE:

- **Adobe Systems**

- **Boeing**

- **Costco**

- **Google**

- **Microsoft**

- **Nordstrom**

- **PCL Construction**

- **Perkins Coie Law Firm**

- **REI Outdoor Equipment**

- **Starbucks Coffee**

- **Whole Foods Market**

WHY WASHINGTON, D.C.?

Population: 592,000 in the city (5.3 million in the greater metro area)

Cost of Living index: 138

Washington, D.C., offers a diversified economy composed of professional and business service jobs as well as federal government operations. According to *Forbes*, despite the recent economic recession, D.C. still ranks second in the country in terms of long-term housing markets. A recent Brookings Institution Study found that the city ranks fourth of the top one hundred metro areas in terms of quality jobs.

Thanks to the well-developed Metrorail subway system, commuting from the suburbs to downtown and back is usually fast and easy. D.C. also offers its residents dozens of historic sites and museums, including the Smithsonian museums and the National Gallery of Art. For those of you James Bond fanatics, there is also an excellent Spy Museum.

In addition to being an interesting place to live, Washington, D.C., has many other strengths. For instance, D.C. boasts an incredibly high level of research and development, including cutting-edge research in health care. The funding for scientists in the region is twice the national average.

Although the district is the center of America's government, it also has many non-government-related businesses in addition to scientific research, such as education, finance, and public policy. It is home to two Fortune 500 companies and is a leader in foreign real estate investment. D.C. also is a leading metro area in high-tech employment.

Another great reason to investigate the nation's capital stems from its preferred position as the epicenter of the country. The D.C. area has received $3.7 billion in contracts, grants, and loans related to the 2009–2010 stimulus package. According to the *Wall Street Journal*, this amount is three times the national average for every resident. The *WSJ* also reports that over $2.2 billion has gone to private firms, many helping in the administration of the stimulus effort.

Several specific firms have received stimulus funds and thus may be adding jobs. For example, Clark Construction Group LLC of Bethesda, Maryland, funded 110 full-time jobs in 2010 after a stimulus award of $161 million for several new construction projects. Clark will construct a Coast Guard building for the Department of Homeland Security in addition to making repairs to the Jefferson Memorial and Andrews Air Force Base. Consulting firm Booz-Allen Hamilton of McLean, Virginia, received $100 million in contracts for government agencies as a result of the stimulus package. Other stimulus fund recipients included Westat Inc., a data research firm in Rockville, Maryland, accounting mega-firm Deloitte, and regional offices of IBM. The stimulus program has also offered funding to nonprofits and trade groups who have been hired to help implement stimulus projects.

BUSINESSES TO INVESTIGATE:

- **Accenture**

- **Booz Allen Hamilton**

- **Capital One**

- **Coventry Health Care Inc.**

- **Daneher Corp**

- **Dyncorp International**

- **Gannett Co.**

- **Harman International Industries Inc.**

- **Juniper Networks**

- **Lockheed Martin**

- **Marriot**

- **MITRE**

- **NetApp**

- **Price Warehouse Coopers**

- **SAP**

- **U.S. Army**

- **W.R. Grace & Co.**

Although urban centers are exciting, you may wish to settle in a more relaxed environment. Recent studies show that several states are fostering great economic growth. These states boast some of the most beautiful landscapes in the country and are thus beautiful places to live. Forbes. com highlights the following five states as best for business and careers: Utah, Virginia, North Carolina, Colorado, and Washington. Forbes analyzed 33 points of data, including business costs, labor supply, regulatory environment, economic climate, and prospects for growth and life quality.

Utah, for example, boasts a growing economy; employment has increased there by 1.5 percent, and household incomes are surging twice as fast as the national average. Many large companies are expanding their presence in Utah, including Goldman Sachs, Adobe, Oracle, and eBay. Virginia continues to show economic growth as well, with low business costs and a thriving economic climate. North Carolina sports a relaxed regulatory environment, as well as low business costs. Colorado shows favorable prospects for growth and a high ranking for quality of life. The state of Washington shows strength in labor supply, growth prospects, and a regulatory environment. In other words, the state government makes it easy for business owners to start and run businesses in Washington. If you ask yourself questions about the life you wish to lead, and your answers point to a place other than a wild and woolly city, you may wish to investigate the opportunities in some of these job growth-oriented states.

CHAPTER TO-DO LIST:
- Take a deep breath; that was a lot of information. Keep in mind that these are the cities we found interesting and worthwhile. Each one has a lot to offer a young person such as yourself, but as we mentioned before, it all comes down to you.
- Use this chapter as an impetus to conduct your own thorough research. Be sure to investigate a city based

on the numerous factors mentioned in this chapter. For instance: would you like to raise a family there? Would it be a fun place to explore? If you got laid off, would you be able to find another job and still enjoy the city?

- Remember: You're going to be married not only to your career, but also to the city you live in. Look before you leap.

CHAPTER TO-DON'T LIST:

- Get the management profiles when researching a company to discover who's who and the mission statement for the firm.
- Google articles from the *WSJ, New York Times,* etc. regarding the firm so you have some insights related to current issues management is facing.
- Don't forego your own research in favor of ours. Even if you find a city in this list that you believe to be the perfect place for you, do your own research to be sure.
- Don't solely investigate the company to which you are applying.
- Don't be afraid to take risks, as long as they are educated risks.

STEP 4

STEP 4:

Brand yourself; polish your skills.

In this chapter we discuss how to "get your foot in the door," as they say, and the ways in which you should package yourself every step of the way. Packaging yourself is different from interviewing in part because it begins much earlier. A candidate for a job does not become an attractive option merely a few weeks before an interview. You can start building credentials as early as high school and college.

Part of this "packaging" process is figuring out how to best showcase yourself and what you bring to any table. Some people call this *practical intelligence*, and others call this *social intelligence*. Whatever name you give this ability, it's a measure of how well you take advantage of social opportunities, regulate your moods, delay momentary gratification in favor of a better long-term result, and empathize with others. If your practical intelligence is up to par, you'll have no problem developing a good professional instinct and social intuition.

Leading experts on intelligence believe that your practical intelligence is a big predictor of your future success. The "brand" you develop for yourself must demonstrate your practical intelligence to those with whom you interview and (hopefully!) with whom you'll work. Practical intelligence comes into play in virtually every interaction you have—it is not just a tool for mapping out your future. For instance, every time you interact with a gatekeeper, you must realize that you are marketing yourself to them. Every phone call, e-mail, interview, discussion, smoke signal, telepathic exchange, etc. is a demonstration of your "brand." You are marketing your brand image by building up an impressive track record of your successes. Ask yourself the following two questions:

"What is it about me that will benefit this college, school, or employer?" and "What exactly does the school or employer need in an applicant to benefit its organization?"

FROM HIGH SCHOOL TO COLLEGE:

In order to get into the college of your choice, you must figure out a way to "package" yourself so that you stand out against every other candidate. You must do a little planning in terms of the way you spend your time in high school. In addition to working hard to get a high GPA and achieving high scores on the SAT and/or ACT, you need to show passionate participation in relevant volunteer and extracurricular activities. In other words, you should show some consistency in your interests and how you have satisfied these interests through the use of your after-school time and summers. You need to market yourself well to get noticed during the application process.

One significant way to demonstrate that you will add value to an incoming freshman class is to show that you have learned valuable, transferable skills through your school, work, or personal experiences. You should discuss these transferable skills in your application essays. If you have the opportunity to interview with an admissions representative or alumni of a prospective college, you should be prepared to showcase these skills as you answer and ask questions.

WHAT ARE TRANSFERABLE SKILLS?

- **Communication skills include:**
  - Editing
  - Expressing ideas
  - Facilitating discussions or meetings
  - Listening
  - Negotiating
  - Presenting
  - Speaking a foreign language
  - Speaking and writing effectively

- **Research and planning skills include:**
  - Analysis
  - Brainstorming
  - Coordinating events
  - Focusing on details
  - Forecasting
  - Goal setting
  - Information gathering
  - Organizing
  - Problem solving
  - Record keeping

- **Interpersonal skills include:**
  - Coaching
  - Conflict resolution
  - Crisis management
  - Delegating responsibility
  - Handling complaints
  - Motivating
  - Team building

- **Leadership skills include:**
  - Dealing with change
  - Decision making
  - Enforcing policies
  - Ethics
  - Implementation
  - Management
  - Persuasion
  - Time management
  - Training

Begin to take an inventory of your transferable skills. You may be surprised how many skills you have developed over the years through your participation in work, volunteering, extra-curricular activities, student government, etc. The idea here is to begin developing a collection of examples that highlight these skills, while looking for more opportunities over time to continue to develop in these areas. You must *show* a college how all of your experiences have helped you acquire some of these very valuable skills that will not only help *you* to succeed in college, but will also help you contribute to the college community.

Colleges and universities are businesses. Each one has a mission statement as well as a culture and a reputation. In that sense, they too have a brand image. How do these schools improve their images? They attract talented students, who upon graduation will join the prestigious alumni and thus add value to the school. Schools are in the business of adding distinction and value to their reputations. This helps them generate capital, which helps them to enlighten and educate *you*! Your school gives to you, and then it becomes your job to give back to your school by *making a difference*. This value could be as simple as inspiring other top students from your field to apply to the school in the future.

It will be helpful for you to be able to *project your added value*. This is a common term used in the business world but applies not only to businesses but also to you as you seek entry to a school or to a company. The idea of added value is basically the idea of what you, and your experiences, will add to the organization. How will you help improve the student body? What diverse experiences will you draw upon to add to the bottom line of the company? What specific strength will you use to help advance a goal of the organization? Only you can answer these questions, and you must think of the answer *before* you interact with a gatekeeper at the place where you want in. For example, during high school you might have volunteered to work with special needs children or perhaps worked at a food bank. In your applications, avoid just listing *experiences*, talk about your passion for giving back to your community, society, and the less fortunate. If you were ever a part of a diverse population, describe how this exposure to diversity shaped you. Most schools value diversity a great deal these days. Your examples should reinforce the idea that *you* will weave richness into the tapestry that is the student population. Always make sure to describe your experiences and skills in a way that makes them applicable to your desired future career.

Colleges favor students who show focus and initiative in pursuing an academic passion. Admissions officers will be impressed with students who demonstrate a clear desire to make a difference in the world. It's important to take into account the perspective of the particular college or university as well as the particular programs they offer that are of interest to you. The key here is to *show* why you are a great candidate for admission—someone who brings a lot to the table and will add value to the school. You may wish to research famous alumni and show how you identify with their agendas or work after leaving the school.

It's also important to make sure that the admissions officers of your first choice school know that their school is your first choice. Explain clearly why this school is your first choice and why you are a great fit. Do your research and learn about the offerings of different departments and professors. One student wished to find a university that featured a notable industrial design program. He also wanted to attend a large university rather than a small arts school. After interviewing a few successful industrial designers and consulting books, such as *The Fiske Guide to Colleges*, he found two prospective schools. His knowledge of the program and his passion for the craft impressed the two admissions offices. Now a student in one of these highly selective programs, he reports that his homework paid off in that he found a great match and differentiated himself from all the other applicants.

You should investigate the academic programs offered at a particular school and be ready to mention those programs in your application to that school. For example, "I look forward to studying political science with Professor X, who worked in the White House," or "I want to participate in the junior year abroad program, continuing my study of

Italian in Florence," or "I want to continue my interest in environmental studies and economics, pursuing a degree in this newly developed joint major." Our advice, as always, is to do your research. You will certainly stand out in a sea of applicants that send one generic response to all prospective colleges.

YOUR MAJOR – A MAJOR DECISION:

Before you market yourself for your first job, you must consider how your academic background will affect your suitability or attractiveness for a particular position. For example, if you plan to pursue a position in international business, perhaps you should consider a dual major in economics and a foreign language. If you are hoping to enter a field involving design, then you should examine whether you want to major in graphic design, product (industrial) design, or software design. The idea is to gather information to make an informed, pragmatic decision about your college major. If you decide to follow your passions and your passions cannot pay the rent, consider a dual major in an area that will stimulate you emotionally, mentally, and fiscally.

One consideration not to overlook is what major most appeals to you. Of course, you may enter school undecided, as many freshmen do. However, you should always take the time to research a school's academic reputation in your areas of interest, as well as the strength of the college in assisting students with future job placement.

Now more than ever, students who are starting college must be aware of what will happen *after* college. In this economy, the question, "How will I ever see a return on this huge investment?" seems to be asked more and more frequently. Because of this recent student emphasis on making money, colleges and universities across the country are seeing a shift in curriculum from more abstract majors, such as philosophy and classics, to more practical majors, such as business, public health, Chinese, Arabic, and many biological sciences. The University of Michigan reports that enrollment in Asian languages is up 38 percent from 2002 while the study of French has dropped five percent. Although budgetary matters drive many course changes, the underlying force is the difficult economy and the tightened job market of this decade.

Many universities are also reporting that a surprising number of incoming freshmen—in some cases as many as 10 percent—have started their own businesses while still in high school! Where colleges once touted the values of a widely based "liberal arts education," many of these institutions now promote internships and job placement. Experts such as Debra Humphreys, president of the Association of American Colleges and Universities, warn, however, that specializing in a niche area is not the only factor that contributes to success; you need to have a good grasp of basic writing and speech skills as well!

Many schools are now focusing on weaving career discussions into classes in every major. For example, the University of Texas aids students by supplying them with a list of possibilities for using their majors in the workplace. The directors of many universities, such as the University of Maryland, offer to help students create their own personal brand. At Babson College, students not only study business in the classroom, they also form corporations, market products, and give presentations in simulated business meetings. As the engine of the local economy, the college or university that you choose will have a strong connection to local industries and businesses. Therefore, pay close attention to the "location, location, location" of said school and its ties to the economy both locally and nationally.

When branding yourself, you should also take into account which major will work best for you in today's economy. Paying close attention to market trends and societal shifts will help guide you to a field that will be both fulfilling *and* lucrative. You may wish to pursue a double major if your academic passion does not show any potential for career promise. Although we all hope that our passions will pay the bills, sometimes we must take a step back and consult professionals in the career guidance department to assess what other major could complement our chosen major to make it more marketable. Another important consideration will be *where* you choose to study and perhaps ultimately live. You will need to investigate the reputations and locations of the schools you are considering in terms of how they assist graduates in your particular area of interest. Are internships available? Does the college or university foster a healthy network of professors, alumni, or companies in your chosen field of study?

When thinking about entering the workforce in the next decade, you should use foresight in choosing a college or university that has strong connections with corporations that are growing and offering jobs to new graduates. A recent article in the *Wall Street Journal* suggests that schools that are willing to partner with corporations for collaborative research often open jobs to new graduates of those schools. For example, according to the article, nearly 2,000 Penn State alumni work at Lockheed Martin, nearly one hundred Penn State faculty members have worked on research projects at Lockheed in the past eight years, and more than 200 Penn State graduates were hired to work for the company in 2009. The *WSJ* further reports that Penn State has entered similar relationships with close to fifty companies since 1995.

Similarly, Arizona State University spotlights engineering students who are working on software for defense contractor Raytheon, Col, while bioengineers from ASU work on radiation equipment for the Mayo Clinic. Purdue University sponsors several research agreements with several companies, such as Rolls Royce. As you research a potential school for undergraduate or graduate work, you should investigate whether you can avail yourself of all the options these relationships allow for research projects, internships, and perhaps eventual employment. Moreover, if you're contemplating a potential market for your first job, you should investigate whether a college or university may in fact be the engine of a local economy—and whether this fact will help fuel the sustainability of the particular location. The idea across the board is to recognize the importance of your potential relationships with professors and their connections with the outside world.

HOW TO TAKE IT TO THE NEXT LEVEL – IS GRADUATE SCHOOL IN THE CARDS? FROM COLLEGE TO GRADUATE SCHOOL:

For many students today, graduate school will be a necessity. Hopefully by this stage in the game you will have established yourself at the perfect college for you with a high GPA as well as some college activities and experiences. By your junior year, you should begin investigating the following:
- Graduate programs (admissions requirements, benefits, requirements, etc.)
- Graduate school exams (LSAT, GMAT, GRE, MCAT, etc.)
- Summer employment (relevant to your field, if possible)

Don't put off researching test dates or studying for these important exams. You might even consider signing up for test prep courses that are offered through a variety of avenues. There are books, classes, tutors, and online help out there for almost all of the major graduate school entrance exams. Be sure to give yourself enough time to study for these tests—two a.m. cram sessions will not suffice! Keep in mind that these tests cost hundreds of dollars, so you will want to do your best the first time around.

At this time in your education, it's important to take full advantage of your school's placement office. Learn as much as you can about the wide spectrum of employment opportunities that will become available to you once you earn your advanced degree. Attending graduate school will most likely help you gain job options that you never knew existed in your field.

Your winter and summer breaks are great opportunities not only to study for these tests, but also to research various companies, industries, areas of interest, etc. Volunteering and interning are two excellent ways to pursue an interest in a given field—and both of these activities look great on a resume (especially the latter). Internships can offer a valuable insider's view into the career you might pursue or the corporate world in general. First-hand experience is the best kind of research you can do about the type of job you might want to have in the future. The skills gained from internships will also go a long way in landing your dream job. Some studies show that 50 percent of students with internship experience receive higher salaries from their first jobs than those who have never completed an internship. Other studies report that 56 percent of interns eventually receive full-time job offers!

Beyond these obvious benefits, many internships are actually paid positions or may count toward college credit work. By bridging the path from academic life to the real world, internships are an enlightening exercise when deciding whether you are meant for a particular career. Moreover, you may learn many beneficial skills that will pay off in the future, such as:
- Conducting surveys
- Dealing with office politics
- Interviewing
- Organizing and publicizing events
- Time management

- Understanding company policies
- Writing press releases

All of these skills will help you as you plan your next step and eventually set foot in "the real world" where your dream job awaits.

WHY INTERNSHIPS ARE THE STEPPING STONE TO FIRST JOBS IN THIS NEW ECONOMY:

A 2010 survey from the National Association of Colleges and Employers found that almost 57 percent of students from the graduating class of 2009 found their first jobs as conversions from internships. Internship recruiting is on the rise.

As a college student, you should take advantage of meet-and-greets and corporate information sessions regarding internships. Across the nation, corporations are drawing from intern pools to full jobs. For example, Boeing Corporation, based in Chicago, offered 250 interns full-time jobs out of the pool of nine hundred-plus summer 2009 interns. The *Wall Street Journal* reports that in 2010, Pricewaterhouse Coopers hired 1,454 rising juniors and seniors for summer internships and that 90 percent of those eligible interns were offered full-time jobs. As the numbers and examples indicate, internships are providing a way to get your foot in the door.

So what does it all come down to? Planning. Planning is an integral part of the college-to-graduate school transition (as well as the rest of your life). You need to assess your academic skills as well as your work experience as you look toward your dream career. Your academic recommendations will also have an impact on your desirability, as will your specific accomplishments and work experience. You must prove to the admissions counselors that you will have used your undergraduate time constructively and creatively. Remember: colleges are looking for evidence that you will be able to succeed in a rigorous, academic graduate program.

- The more information you have about a particular area of interest, the better decisions you will make for your future. If you work in a law firm as a legal assistant, in an advertising agency as an assistant to an executive, or as a research assistant in a hospital laboratory, you should be able to answer the following questions at the end of your experience:
- Can I envision myself working long hours in this environment?
- Do I find pleasure in learning more about this field?
- Do the people who work here have time for families and outside interests?
- Do the people who work here seem unusually stressed out, overburdened, and/or overextended?
- Would I want to be in the employees' shoes? Would I be comfortable with the demands of their jobs and their compensation?

Try to put yourself in the shoes of the people you observe. Think about whether or not you could see yourself holding a similar position in five or ten years from now. If not, it might be worthwhile to look into some other jobs or areas for which you might be better suited. Why try to get a job that you're not going to be happy with? It makes sense to spend the extra time now to find out whether or not a particular career is right for you.

FROM COLLEGE AND/OR GRADUATE SCHOOL TO YOUR FIRST JOB:

So you have your degree in hand (undergraduate, graduate, or both) and now you are in the market for a career. You are working through the career planning strategies set forth in this book. Again, studying is the key to making good decisions at this step in the process. You should explore all of your options while you still have the time and flexibility to do so. Without an existing career or family, you have the freedom to move around and take chances. We want to make sure that you make informed decisions that have been the product of a great deal of exploration of your options and personal reflection. Are you able to move away from home and, if so, is that something that you want?

Are you planning to stay in the area you consider "your home turf" or move away? There are some good reasons to stay close to where you grew up or where you went to college. For starters, hopefully you have built a good name in your community. You may also have developed a large body of professional contacts through networking (we will go into this further in the next section). Although you may want to experience a new place, don't underestimate the perks of staying in your preexisting comfort zone. Keep in mind: there is a possibility that upon graduation you may *have to* return home until the economy regenerates. This is normal. Many of your peers are stuck in the same predicament.

With that in mind, we also suggest that you open your mind to the possibility of moving to a new location that has industries to sustain jobs in your field. As discussed in the previous chapter, there are a lot of factors to consider in terms of your overall quality of life when choosing a new city. For example, if a warm climate is important to you and you're looking for a job in high-tech industries, you might want to start your search in Austin, Houston, or Atlanta for potential homes. Those areas are sizzling in temperature as well as the high-tech industry! Don't discount your personal needs and wants when looking for employment. The highest paying job will not necessarily lead to the highest quality of life. Again, the theme we keep enforcing is: *look before you leap*; take a careful, researched look into what you want out of life, what you want to do, who you want to be, and where you want to live before making any finite decisions.

"GATEKEEPERS": WHO ARE THEY AND WHAT DO THEY DO?

The gatekeepers mentioned earlier in this chapter are the key influencers and decision makers who determine whether you get in, move up, or move on. This illustrious group may include (but is not limited to) your parents, high school teachers, school administrators, college professors, bosses, or any heads of organizations where you've worked or spent time. Throughout your life, you should be mindful of who these people are and how you can earn their respect during the time you spend with them. These individuals may hold the keys to the entrance of the school where you are seeking admission or the job you seek to acquire. Remember that they will be judging you on:

- Academic performance
- Adaptability to new circumstances
- Communications
- Congeniality

- Effectiveness as a team player
- Effectiveness as a leader
- Overall social intelligence
- Track record in job performance
- Willingness to take the initiative

You need to show these gatekeepers that you are capable of making the right decisions and adding value to their particular causes or institutions.

NETWORKING – THE KEY TO YOUR FUTURE:

From the time you enter high school, networking should be in the back of your mind. You should never stop networking. Success can often be determined by your opportunities, and those opportunities may likely arise through people you know. The importance of networking increases even more once you start college. Your professors may be able to open the gates to research and internship opportunities. They can also write letters of recommendation for you—assuming you make a good impression, of course! Your contacts in college may turn out to be gatekeepers in the future.

Networking allows you to form allegiances with people who will aid you enormously in your search for a career—not to mention your advancement in said career. Many sources, included us, stress that networking is one of the most productive sources for landing a job. The reason networking is such a powerful job-hunting tool is the fact that your network will give you access to a "hidden job market." The hidden job market is composed of employment opportunities that have not yet become known to the general public; although these jobs exist, they have not yet been advertised.

The message is simple: *gain the respect of your employers and professors.* Eventually they will be the ones you need to call on for references and leads. This is not the time to be shy. If you have made a great impression on these gatekeepers, then now is the time to ask them for help in making important introductions. You have become a "known quantity," and typically your chances of being hired will be far greater than if you were someone random who just walked in off the street. A candidate that a hiring manager is familiar with is more likely to be given careful consideration than a stranger or someone who lacks a personal referral. Use your social, volunteer, work, and academic network for assistance in finding employment. There is no shame in taking advantage of the opportunities that people who are close to you provide.

NETWORKING AND SOCIAL MEDIA – LINK IN TO LINKEDIN:

Many college and graduate students turn to social media for feedback and assistance in resolving many issues related to the job hunt and networking. This is because there are many helpful ways to use social media in your job search. First of all, when it comes to resumes, several useful tools are available online:

- Razume.com – a community that will help you build your resume and then give you feedback from other users in the community. There is also an online job search option.

- ResumeSocial.com – a social resume community where users review your cover letters. There is also a career center with a wealth of valuable information.
- VisualCV.com – a site that will assist you in creating a resume and uploading audio, video, or portfolio items to augment your presentation. The user can adjust the layout and then download the result as a PDF file to print or e-mail.

The website LinkedIn is also profoundly useful. LinkedIn offers a quick and easy means to make connections with other professionals in your area of expertise. It works on a system of degree—the first degree being those who you know personally, through a direct connection. The second-degree network members are people who know at least one member of your first-degree network. Third-degree members are those—as you have probably already figured out—who know at least one person in your second-degree network. LinkedIn essentially creates a spider's web of people who are all connected through each other's contacts. Here are just a few of the things you can do with LinkedIn:

- Ask for informational interviews
- Connect with hiring managers
- Find jobs on the LinkedIn job board
- Gain more credibility through your connections' recommendations of you
- Make connections within a company to get tips on applying for a particular position
- Market yourself through various groups and organizations
- Post an online resume
- Research a company before an interview

- Take advantage of your status as an alumnus of the university you attended (most schools have LinkedIn groups)

There are many privacy settings that you can manipulate in order to limit the types of requests others may use to approach you. You can choose to be open or closed to: career opportunities, expertise requests, consulting offers, business deals, new ventures, personal reference requests, job inquiries, and general requests to connect. As you can see, there are many possibilities with this social networking site. There are even tools such as the JobInsider browser toolbar that keeps track of the jobs you search for on search engines such as Monster or Career Builder. JobInsider then lets you know if anyone from those companies is a member of LinkedIn. All basic LinkedIn accounts are free to anyone eighteen years or older. There are paid accounts that allow intro-mail messages, ability to view more detailed profiles, and reference searches.

The previous functions of LinkedIn are only the beginning as it can be used in numerous other ways as well. For example: answering questions or asking intriguing questions in your field through LinkedIn Answers can build your credibility and visibility among other networkers. Make certain that you think out your responses, fact check, and proofread before posting *anything*. Don't be a self-promoter; realize that you may need to be giving and helpful to other users before reaping any personal gain. You can let people know you're searching for work, though limit how frequently you do this and think about how to best word these requests. Job seekers can also look for groups for entrepreneurs and investors who may be aware of exciting new job opportunities.

We would recommend using this site, and any website or resource that helps you meet new professionals and market yourself to potential employers. The *WSJ* also suggests creating a profile with freelance job boards like Odesk.com, Guru.com, and Elance.com to get your talent noticed. This part of your process is about building relationships. You have done your personal best—you have not settled for mediocrity, so demonstrate this to others.

The Interview:
Your Opportunity Day – How to Get There and What to do When You Are There.

Now that you've decided on an industry that satisfies your skills and wants and chosen a place to live, it's time to begin looking for the ideal job for you. In order to hook and reel in your dream job, you'll need to be able to give a phenomenal interview. This chapter will teach you how to land an interview and prepare for *your* opportunity day.

In order to be invited to interview for a given position, you must first grab the attention of the company's hiring manager or a corporate recruiter. One way to become an obvious candidate for a job is to post your resume on general, industry, and function-specific job boards. Submitting your resume directly to a company when a position that matches your background becomes available is also a great way to get noticed. Keep in mind that if you are submitting your resume directly to a company, you should include a cover letter that will differentiate you from the other candidates. Your letter should convey what makes you special. Here is a step-by-step guide to putting your best letter forward:

CLEAR, CONCISE COVER LETTERS:

As you prepare this very important document, think of the following statement: "I must show, not tell, why I am the right candidate for the job." There are thousands of examples of cover letters online and in books. Although models are helpful, each job and each candidate are unique. Thus we opted to give you some guidelines as you construct a cover letter for each new job prospect.

- **The Address Line:** Always address a specific person, if possible. This may take some research, but do not say "Dear Sir or Madam" or "To Whom It May

Concern." If you cannot find the name of the person, then you may address to "X Corporation, Human Resources Director," or "Hiring Manager and RE: X position."

- **Introductory sentence:** Use a personalized, straightforward introductory sentence. Do not try to be clever or cute. If you can mention someone or some group that led you to this job opportunity, all the better.

    For example, "At the suggestion of _____ (a person, a college office, a recruiter), I am applying for _____."

- **Next sentence:** Flatter the company! Use an enthusiastic tone to show how your interest and passion match the company's history or goals. "I have long-admired your_____" or "I am excited to hear that you are hiring in connection with your new venture." If you can't add this sentence, don't worry. This is not supposed to make you sound insincere, but merely to show that you know about the company's history, reputation, or current situation.

- **Next paragraph:** Communicate why your experience initiative/skills/adaptability make you a great candidate for this job.

    Example: "As a _____ at the University of _____, I was responsible for _____." Or: "Working at _____ taught me how to be _____ and _____. I am eager to apply that _____ and _____ to this position (or opportunity)."

A FEW NEVERS:

NEVER send out your resume without a cover letter

NEVER discuss why you need the job to build your resume or for financial reasons

NEVER address the letter to the company

NEVER trust spell/grammar check as your only proofreading device

NEVER use the casual language of e-mailing and texting

- **Ending:** Thank the person for his/her time. Example: "Thank you for your consideration. I will follow up with you in the coming week." Or: "I look forward to hearing from you soon."
- **Closing**: Use something simple like Sincerely, Best, Thank you.
- **PROOFREAD!** Get help! You do not want a typo or a grammatical error on this first impression piece. Date and save a copy for your files. If you're not sending a hard copy of the cover letter and instead are using e-mail, consider sending the cover letter in the text of the e-mail rather than as an attachment. Why not make it easy on the prospective employer? Your resume can be sent as an attachment. *Caution:* Try to make it a habit to wait to fill in the TO: line of the e-mail address until you're 100 percent certain that the cover letter is error free. Another good idea is to send the letter to yourself first. Print out the letter to make sure that the formatting is correct.

You need an amazing resume to attach to your cover letter. Although educating you on effective resume creation is not our main priority here, we feel that it is important to discuss a few key points to keep in mind while you're writing your resume. Your resume will not only play a large part in earning you an interview; it will serve as the interviewer's first impression of you. In an article called "Advice on Giving Advice to 20-Year-Olds," Jeffrey Zaslow suggests that you also make an e-friendly showcase of your talents. He writes: "Young people today are often better off networking on social media or creating a website to display their talents, with videos and samples of their work." This is not to say that you should forego creating a resume. Resumes are critical in making a good first impression. *Always make a great first impression.* The following list contains the five critical tips for crafting a stellar resume:

1. Be Straightforward

You do not want your resume to be an incoherent mess! Face it: sometimes it's not easy to talk about yourself. That's why a resume is so important. It's an opportunity to show a potential employer, in a straightforward and organized way, exactly who you are and what you have accomplished. List your history in *relevant* categories. For example, list education, skills, employment, volunteerism, and so on. You will not use the exact same version of your resume for each position that you apply for; actually, you will want to be flexible with your resume so that you can tailor it to the needs of each company and position. Regardless, your resume should always be straightforward, organized, and honest.

2. Work Toward a Particular Goal

Be sure to keep your ultimate goal in mind when writing a resume, which is to convince a hiring specialist that you will help his or her company in achieving its goals. Carefully select items that reflect *pertinent, relevant experiences* to include in your resume. It's a good idea to include non-work-related activities and achievements *if* they have some impact or implications on your job pursuit. For example: imagine that you are seeking a job in development, fundraising, or marketing. Perhaps in college you played an important role in fundraising activities for your school or a charity. This would be an excellent experience to include in your resume since it shows your leadership ability as well as your capacity to support and benefit an organization. *In short, include resume items that speak to your capability to add value to the company.*

3. Delay Discussion of Salary Requirements

Do not mention anything about salary or benefit requirements on your resume. If you do, you will be giving the impression that you are either "all about show me the money" or that you would be a high-maintenance employee. There is a proper time to discuss such things, but it is usually later in the process; namely, sometime during the interview process or if the employer specifically requests the information. Keep it in mind, but wait until it comes up in conversation.

4. Explain Each Entry

Make every word of this crucial document count. Write simple but detailed descriptions of your prior jobs and education to emphasize your successes, experiences, and acquired skills. You will also want to use these entries to tell your potential employer about your character traits (we will address these later in the chapter).

5. Proofread, Proofread, Proofread!

This is your first—and only—opportunity to make an excellent first impression. Don't ruin your chances to make a good first impression with misspelled words, capitalization errors, and silly syntactical mistakes. Read through the document aloud once or twice in order to catch more errors. Also, always have a second set of eyes look over your resume to proofread it and make sure that it flows. Remember how your English teachers always told you that errors cause you to lose credibility with your reader? Well, that is exactly the situation with your resume. Proofread! Then proofread again!

There is one more thing to keep in mind when building your resume: if you are still in college, most universities have a career services center that offers help with resume crafting. Use these centers as a resource to produce the best resume possible. If your college does not have such a mecca of aid, it more than likely has a writing center where you can get someone to check your resume for spelling and mechanics. Often the individuals at these centers can be very helpful in "beefing up" your resume or, in other words, using your work and school experience to match what the potential employer is looking for.

RESUME TOOLBOX:

1. Brainstorm first. Make a list of everything you've done for at least the last four years. Include education, paid positions, internships, athletic activities, volunteer work, school activities, community work, and hobbies.

2. The resume/format should make your particular information shine. Your contact information goes at the top. Include your e-mail. Don't refer to yourself as Mr. or Ms. For most recent college graduates, the **Education** section goes next, followed by **Experience, Skills**, and **Interests**. Resumes generally fall into three categories: Chronological, Functional, and Combination. Chronological lists jobs in reverse chronological order. Functional focuses on skills and experience; this is particularly useful for gaps in employment history. Combination resumes list skills and experience and then employment history.

3. **Education:** colleges attended, degrees attained, any honors awarded

   Experience: work or internship history. List company/business/firm, location, dates of employment, positions held, and a bulleted list of your responsibilities and achievements Example: Marketing Assistant, AD USA, Cleveland, OH, Summers 2002–2004. Prioritize the information you offer by placing yourself in your potential employer's position: what will help you get this particular job? Quantify as much as you can with dollars, percentage, and numbers.

Skills: If pertinent to the particular position, use key words to make your explanations as concise as possible. Edit out pronouns (I) and articles (the, a) and begin phrases with verbs. See the list below for help with clear, exciting language.

Interests: Include these if they will be a great "hook" for later interviewing

4. Limit your resume to one page. Choose your words carefully.

5. If you e-mail your resume, make sure that the document tag line is clear and helpful: Smith Resume for Position X, per _____.

6. **Great Language for Resumes**: Accomplished, accelerated, achieved, assessed, audited, addressed, administered, broadened, capacity, chaired, clarified, communicated, competence, conceived, consistent, coordinated, counseled, created, designed, devised, developed, diagnosed, drafted, effected, ensured, established, executed, expedited, explained, extended, formulated, founded, global, implemented, improved, innovated, insured, interpreted, involved, investigated, launched, maturity, meditated, monitored, motivated, navigated, negotiated, participated, planned, potential, prepared, procured, productive, proficient, profitable, proposed, proven, pursued, raised, reconciled, recruited, redesigned, reduced, replaced, represented, resourceful, responsible, revamped, reviewed, revised, saved, shaped, shared, significant, sold, specified, stable,

streamlined, strengthened, stressed, succeeded, tackled, targeted, taught, tested, thorough, trained, tripled, tutored, umpired, unified, unraveled, updated, utilized, verified, versatile, vigorous, weighted, won, worked, wrote...

WHO IS A REFERENCE? WHAT CAN YOU DO TO ENSURE THAT YOU HAVE GOOD REFERENCES?

References are usually required for jobs. Employers need to be able to verify your information. Did you really work there? Did you really master those skills and subjects? How do you relate to others?

You should provide references on a separate sheet of paper. You should consider professors, former employers, and basically any adult who can speak highly of your character and work, including internships and volunteer positions. Family friends, peers, and family physicians are usually not appropriate options. Remember, these people will be asked about your ability to work with others, take directions, honesty, reliability, productivity as well as your demeanor and attitude. If you don't have any relevant references, get busy! Get involved in an internship or volunteer group in a field relative to your respective employment, and cultivate a relationship that will lead to a glowing reference. If you have journeyed through reverse career path planning, then you will have some helpful ideas of where to start.

Smart candidates will be strategic with their choice of references. These people should not only know you well, but also have information about you that is relevant to your prospective employers. You should choose individuals who are good responders to e-mails and phone calls.

HOW DO I ASK FOR A RECOMMENDATION?

If you don't see this person on a regular basis, then you may need to reintroduce yourself via e-mail or a telephone call. Give busy people enough time to respond. In other words, don't wait until the last minute to gather your references. Make an effort to get to know supervisors and to get a written referral or recommendation *before* you leave the situation. You can always update an old acquaintance as you accomplish bigger and better things.

First, introduce yourself, "I am from _____ How are you?"

Then state what you are applying for and ask, "May I use you as a reference?" Once the person agrees, ask whether e-mail or telephone is the best way to communicate.

Lastly, thank the person and suggest that you will send your resume and a brief description of the job you are seeking. Ask if there is anything else that the person may need from you in order to write the reference.

Make this whole process easy on the reference— include a stamped, addressed envelope to make things more convenient.

IF YOU ARE ASKED TO WRITE ONE FOR THE REFERENCE TO SIGN:

Give the specifics of when you worked for this person and what you did there or how this person got to know you. Give the details of what you accomplished, focusing on your outstanding achievements as you handled particular situations or took initiative. Include some comments from co-workers to back up the assessment.

LAYING THE GROUNDWORK FOR AN AMAZING RECOMMENDATION, OR ALWAYS BE ON YOUR "A" GAME:

When participating in a volunteer project, an internship, or a work position, keep a running record of all the tasks that you successfully complete, as well as all of your written or creative work. You can use these documents to help you as you build your resume, write your cover letters, or give your references some tangible support for your letter of recommendation.

Moreover, keep in mind as you handle each work experience, internship, or volunteer project that you must accept full responsibility for yourself and your actions. No one is perfect—if you botch a job, lose a document, or miss a deadline, admit your error and *make it right as soon as possible*. You will earn the respect of your elders that way. Making excuses or shrugging your shoulders will leave one sort of impression; taking responsibility for the mistake and making corrections will leave a much better one. Remember: a reference will be asked not only specific questions about your skills and knowledge, but also your social skills—how you write, how you interact with others, how you respond on the telephone. The reference may also be asked if you meet deadlines, if you are punctual, if you do whatever it takes to complete a job to the best of your ability, if you are dependable about even showing up to work. Finally, if your new job requires teamwork, your references may be asked about your interactions with colleagues, customers, and superiors. Your references may be asked how you respond to criticism, to instructions, or whether you always need direction. Every step you take now can be a positive step toward a productive future.

DON'T FORGET TO SEND A HAND-WRITTEN THANK YOU NOTE:

A hand-written thank you note is the bare minimum to thank someone. You may wish to do more if you are close to this person. Keep in contact with your reference—even if you don't get the particular job. Let the person know that you would be very grateful for any future openings in the field that he or she may suggest.

HOW TO WRITE A REFERENCE SHEET:

Your reference sheet should be a clean, typo-free, accurate list:

Your Name

Your Address

Telephone, E-mail

REFERENCES:

Name

Company

Position

E-mail

Telephone number

Name

Company

Position

E-mail

Telephone number

PERSONAL MEETINGS:

If you are granted the opportunity to meet with a corporate recruiter or a member of the company to which you are applying, then you must make the most of the opportunity. Take inventory of your transferrable skills (discussed in chapter four) and use them during your job search. Discussing these skills in your cover letter as well as your resume reinforces the claim that the skills you possess are marketable and applicable to a given job.

No matter who your interviewer is you must recognize that this person is a gatekeeper. It's your job to dazzle this gatekeeper. From your initial contact over the phone or e-mail to the assessment he or she makes of your online resume, this gatekeeper is the first screener of your potential. Prepare yourself to wow this first gatekeeper by researching the company as thoroughly as possible before your interview. Here are a few basic tips that some of the country's top corporate recruiters suggest for making a great first impression:

- You must be prepared to talk intelligently about the company and what it does. This includes a familiarity with products, locations, and any newsworthy events concerning the company. This "homework" will show that you are seriously interested in securing a position there.
- Prepare for each interview separately. Be able to explain how your qualifications will fulfill the requirements and expectations of each open position to which you are applying. You must be able to show how your specific skill set will fulfill the needs of the

given company. Be ready to show how you will add value to this organization. Remember, you want this gatekeeper to pull for you throughout this process and to believe in the product you are selling: *you*! Merely demonstrating to the gatekeeper that you are competent is *not enough*. The purpose of this interview is to demonstrate why you are a necessary asset to this company.

- Dress professionally whenever you meet with the recruiter. It's always better to be more conservatively dressed than too casual. You don't want to come off as an over-seller, but you do want to show that you passionately want to obtain this job.

- If you're the fortunate individual to land the job, then the corporate recruiter will assist in the negotiation process. As with every area of job seeking, honesty is always the best policy when discussing compensation. Many companies will seek to verify your prior compensation, even on special projects. You should be honest with your recruiter about the status of interviews with other companies (if you are so lucky to be in this position). If you have a deadline, a recruiter may be able to influence a company to make a faster decision. Furthermore, if you decide that this particular position is not for you, then you should be frank and inform the recruiter as soon as possible. Preserving your integrity and good standing with the person who initially interviewed you will help you to be considered for future positions.

Keep in mind that while it's important to demonstrate your desire for the position, harassing the recruiter with an onslaught of phone calls is ill advised. While it's perfectly acceptable for you to contact the interviewer on a weekly basis, you may reduce your chances of landing the job if you become a nuisance. Interviewers want to meet you and observe you to figure out whether you will mesh with the people and culture that make up their particular organization. The interview is your chance to demonstrate that "Yes—I fit in here!"

As you will learn from your research, people often take interesting paths to reach positions of prominence within a firm or company. The more you know about the people that you will be joining, the better job you can do of assessing whether or not you share a community of interests or backgrounds. Although it seems obvious to many, it's worth stating here that you should not assume anything about your interviewer. Don't be foolish and mention anything that may offend the interviewer, even inadvertently. There are horror stories of college grads who have assumed that interviewers are liberal, conservative, fans of a particular sports team, ardent feminists…You get the picture. Be yourself, but don't assume you should share everything with everybody or that the interviewer shares your value system. Be very careful with your word choice. Don't put your foot in your mouth while you are trying to get a foot in the door!

Another important aspect of the interview is to stress that you want *this* job in *this* city. With the turbulent economy, more and more grads are locating their first jobs in new cities. Reassure your interviewer that you are ready, willing, and able to move to this new place. If you have a built in support system of friends and/or family, share this information. If you have picked up and moved at any time in your school life, let this be known. If you are independent, excited with new options, and eager to start your life in this new, sustainable location, then you should say so. Above all, ask for this job. The interviewer doesn't want to hear that this is the only viable option for you. This is the job you want and where you want to be for the long haul. If you're considering more education, don't talk about this in the interview. If you're told about a company program that supports advanced degree work, of course you should express interest. However, the interview is not the time to cast doubt that you're here to make the company's investment in you pay off.

To prepare for an interview, try to do a dry run with a person you trust. Bounce your ideas back and forth with someone who has either interviewed people for jobs or someone who has been successful in the interviewing process. Be yourself, but show your best qualities. Many interviewers report that sincere, authentic candidates win them over. You must impress your interviewers without coming off as a narcissist. Practice with family, friends, and even self-recordings to develop your confidence.

DO NOT UNDERESTIMATE THE POWER OF A GREAT HANDSHAKE:

When you meet or greet someone, extend a full hand out to shake. Shake with your entire hand, not just your fingers. Use enough force to show that you are serious about this encounter. Shake once, twice, even three times. However, four times is weird, and five times is just creepy. You should strive to look a person square in the eyes. If you have trouble doing this, stare immediately above the eyes, at the person's forehead. You will appear to be looking at the person directly.

MIND YOUR MANNERS WHILE DINING:

If you've been raised by parents who taught you to place your napkin in your lap, to wait for everyone to be served before you eat your food, to take one bite at a time, and to not speak and chew at the same time, then great for you in your journey to become employed! If you haven't been so fortunate, then you should investigate the basics of good manners *before* you share a meal with a prospective employer. At a minimum, consider the following:

- Order conservatively—never order a more expensive meal than your host/hostess.
- Speak politely to the servers; say please and thank you.
- Place your napkin in your lap.
- Don't come hungry—eat something before you show up so you don't devour the bread bowl.
- Take small bites and chew quietly.
- Don't speak with food in your mouth.
- Wipe your mouth often as you eat.
- Learn the proper cutlery to use for soup (the large tablespoon). If you dare order soup, learn how to eat it properly (slide the spoon toward the back of the bowl, lift straight up, then lean forward and quietly sip, not slurp, the contents).
- Break bread over your bread plate before taking a bite. (Your bread plate is always the one on your left).

- Use the small salad fork for salad and the large dinner fork for your meal.
- Learn the proper placement of your cutlery while eating and to signal that you are finished eating
- Say thank you!

MAKE YOURSELF MEMORABLE AND ATTRACTIVE WHEN YOUR OPPORTUNITY DAY ARRIVES:

So now you have finished your resume, sent it to a company with an open position, made your check-up call, and...they want to see you for an interview! Since you don't have the job yet, we advise against a full-scale celebration—but a private victory dance would be more than acceptable. Despite the fact that getting an interview is not an outright job offer, you should still commend yourself on this achievement.

After you are done patting yourself on the back, you need to begin to prepare for the interview. Remember how much you prepared for entering college or graduate school? You need to put just as much time and energy into this important milestone. *The key to nailing an interview is your preparation.*

Once again, we want to reiterate the theme of *being valuable* to your employer. Thus you must emphasize *how you can add value and be a productive asset to the company.* Your prospective employer has a specific need, a definite gap that you are attempting to fill. Figure out what that need is. Investigate who is managing the company and what challenges the business might be facing now. There is an abundance of information online and it is critical for you to know about the company's products, locations, and recent news as well as issues they may be facing where your skills would be beneficial to them. Construct a persuasive case for how your interests, skills, and energy will help the company resolve its issues favorably.

The interview process allows you to tell the company that you have an understanding of its strengths, missions, and culture. You can research the company's needs through public records, Google searches (or your preferred search engine), previous employees, and professional organizations.

One of your main goals during an interview should be to distinguish yourself from other applicants. You do this by making yourself not only *attractive,* but also *memorable.* In many subtle ways—and in some direct ways—you want to exhibit not only your skills, but your character traits as well. If you are a rapid learner or have great listening skills, use the interview to display your best character traits that are relevant to closing the deal and getting the job. Here is a list of traits to consider. Perhaps you have overlooked some strengths that may be beneficial to note in your interviews:

- Well informed (about the company)
- Desire to add value to the firm
- A team player/leader (a true leader puts the team before individual needs)
- Passion for the job
- Amicability
- Problem solver
- Endurance
- Social intelligence

- Articulation
- Resiliency
- Highly focused
- Organized
- Loyalty
- Willingness to learn from others
- Passion for your work
- Adaptability
- Ability to overcome objections (critical if you are in sales)
- Highly motivated

You want to demonstrate these qualities in the interview to show the interviewer that you have *social intelligence*. You can use words like "we" or "our" to infer that you are already employed there. You don't want to appear arrogant, but show them that you would fit in well with their team.

The best way to subtly get the point across that you possess these qualities is to pick four or five of them and address them in some sort of story or anecdote. For instance, by telling a story about a time when you spent days writing and preparing a speech to give upon your favorite professor's resignation, you're demonstrating to the interviewer that you are *loyal, focused,* and *passionate*. If the speech was well received, you can stress your *good articulation*.

Make a point to *show* the interviewer how you can incorporate these traits into your work. Don't just say, "I'm an organized person." First of all, without any supporting evidence, he or she has no reason to believe you. Second of all, a blunt statement such as this one could make you sound arrogant and overly confident. This is especially true with some of the other virtues, like being a leader or loyal to the company. *Show these character traits by using your experience and your history to prove your character.* Use concrete examples of when you demonstrated leadership qualities. You should even go to your interview with a business-style binder, pad of paper, a pen, and a few copies of your resume to show your interviewer that you are organized. Why tell your interviewer that you are organized when your actions can prove it? Remember: actions speak louder than words. You want to "brand" yourself with these positive character traits.

Social intelligence is a major character trait that employers like to see in candidates. If you can interact well with others, you can do a lot for a company. For example, an old college roommate recently called Beth after 20 years of no contact. While Beth was building a career and raising a family, her long-lost friend, Barbara, was in Kenya running African safaris! Barbara was always Miss Sociable in college—meeting with people all the time, life of the party, always interesting to talk with. She began sponsoring an orphanage in Kenya with money she raised in New York. When she visited the orphanage, Barbara was appalled to see the awful, dirty conditions the children were living in, despite the beautiful new clothes she had gotten for them. What did she do? She used her social intelligence to meet with all of her contacts, her friends, her networks, and within a short period of time, she had raised enough money in donations to "adopt" every one of the 50 children in that orphanage to improve their quality of life. How exactly did Barbara inspire her friends? She went out to lunch and told her story to a different person every day, and slowly but surely, each person found her story so heartening that they too were inspired to participate in sponsoring a child.

The amazing thing is she never had to outright ask anyone for a single cent. Barbara merely showed each person pictures of the children she had met who were in need of sponsors. Her enthusiasm and empathy for their plight had the effect of "turning on" her many friends, which caused them to explore how they too could help these beautiful children. One by one, Barbara explained, her friends asked, "How can I help? Can I be a sponsor too?"

Because Barbara is compelling, exuberant for life, likeable, and passionate about her cause, people find her—and thus her cause—difficult to resist. People will support you if they *like you*. The orphanage was Barbara's life force. Half of Barbara's battle to raise support for her cause was something that came naturally to her; she just had to be a good friend. If you develop a broad network of trusting friends, they will want to do business with and support you—even if they don't support your cause.

Barbara's extraordinary social acumen combined with her sincere commitment to her cause enabled her to influence her friends in an almost organic and effortless way. This true story is an example of how a person can inspire others to join a cause or project purely through enthusiasm. You first must show your own commitment to the endeavor and then discern what would interest the person you are seeking to inspire. Show the people you are wooing how they too can make a difference. Plus, through engaging in the project together, you ultimately strengthen your bond with the people who choose to help you. You can easily see how businesses would want to capitalize on this kind of character trait.

Think back to the entrance essay questions from some of the top universities mentioned in the first chapter. Remember how they were focused on the character traits of their potential students? They weren't so much looking for someone with one hundred fifty hours of volunteer service; they were looking for a person whose one hundred fifty hours of volunteer service helped him or her to become a great leader as well as a person with great adaptability. Admissions offices, interviewers, and other gatekeepers will focus on the qualities that you have obtained through your experience. Employers will consistently choose the person who exhibits social intelligence combined with innate ability over the person who has a high IQ but lacks practical interpersonal skills.

TIPS FOR THE PHONE INTERVIEW:

Sometimes pre-screening of candidates is done by telephone. If you're applying for an out-of-state job or a telecommuting position, the initial interviews may be done over the phone as a matter of necessity. Check out the following tips in order to have a successful phone interview:

1. **Find a quiet place for the interview**. Try to schedule the interview for a precise time when your environment will be silent and free of distractions.

2. **Speak even more slowly and clearly than when you are face-to-face**. Also, if you are

having a hard time hearing your interviewer for any reason, blame it on your phone by saying, "I'm so sorry, I'm having a hard time hearing you. Perhaps there's a problem with the volume on my phone."

3. **Use a landline if possible.** Cell phone service is risky and unpredictable. You don't want to constantly be asking, "Can you hear me now? No? How about now?" If you don't have a landline, then stay in an area where your cell phone service is strongest.

4. **Keep all your paperwork in front of you.** This means a copy of your resume, notes to answer anticipated questions, a pen and paper to take notes, and anything else that you think will ensure your success.

5. **Don't eat or drink or chew gum while interviewing on the phone!** Do, however, eat something before your interview to help charge your brain and prevent those embarrassingly loud stomach rumblings.

6. **Maintain your sense of professionalism, and be aware that your facial expressions can't be seen, so don't say anything that requires facial interpretation.** Now is not the appropriate time to ask, "Is your refrigerator running?"

During your job search, you will more than likely have at least a few phone interviews, some more formal than others. Treat any phone conversation with a potential employer as an interview. If you do get the opportunity to meet the interviewer face-to-face, you will have already laid a strong foundation of professionalism.

THE FIRST TEN MINUTES OF THE INTERVIEWING PROCESS:

Some experts believe that the first ten minutes of an interview define the entire encounter. During these first few moments, you will be under extra-intense scrutiny, so you need to blow the interviewer away from the second you enter the room. Here are some behaviors to practice before the interview. Master these steps to give yourself the edge:

- Turn off your cell phone—do not put it on vibrate, do not put it on silent— turn it off. An over-active cell phone is not a good way to start any relationship, especially during a job interview!
- Make good eye contact with the interviewer, especially when answering questions.
- Be an active listener—nod and take notes, if appropriate.
- Be as natural and comfortable as possible. Try not to appear as though you are trying too hard. This could be misinterpreted as meaning you're insincere. You need to project that you are sincerely interested in this particular job.
- Don't just share the ways in which you are competent. Companies are looking for employees who can solve problems and add value. They want to know specifics.
- Avoid sounding arrogant in overstating your skills or abilities. Don't oversell yourself or exaggerate.
- Show a general interest and passion for the job.

- Give a firm handshake and wear a genuine, nice smile. After all, you are never fully dressed without a smile!

ELEVEN STEPS TO AN AWESOME INTERVIEW:

You're bound to be nervous as you approach this big day. Take a deep breath. The more you prepare, the more at ease you will be. Take this list one step at a time, and do some run-throughs with your family, friends, or even a mirror. Remember that interviewing for *any* position will help you prepare for your interview with *the* position you truly want. The general advice is to be confident, yet not over-confident. This will show the interviewer that you are the right candidate for the job and that you want it *today*.

1. **Learn As Much As You Can About the Company and the Position**

   - **Who** is the competition?
   - **What** is the core business or niche this company specializes in?
   - **Why** are your skill sets the right fit for this company?
   - **Where** are the opportunities for growth with this company, in this industry?
   - **How long** has this company been in business?
   - **When** is this market emerging—now and/or in the future?
   - **What** are the responsibilities of this position?
   - **What** skills are involved in doing this job?

These are some of the questions you'll want to know the answers to *before* the interview. Research the company as well as the position for which you're applying. Start with the company's philosophy and mission statement. Carefully read the management profiles and chairman's statement, which should be on the company's website. Utilize outside sources to figure out how others perceive the company. If the company is publicly traded, then look at DowJones.com or Hoover.com to analyze "the numbers." You may also want to track down the company's annual report. Use resources like LinkedIn and those listed at the end of this book to learn as much as possible about the firm's clients and market position. Search the business sections of national newspapers such as the *New York Times* and *Wall Street Journal*.

2. Figure Out How Your Skills Relate to What the Company Needs

Although we have already (albeit briefly) addressed this topic, it is critical that you fully grasp the information. This is where you must be truly honest with yourself. What can you offer this company to help it achieve its goals? How will *your* skills and character traits translate into tangible assets for your employers? Approach the interview the way an insider would: address how your contribution will make a positive difference in the company. Use concrete examples and be as specific as you can.

For example, if you have motivated people to participate in a cause that you believe in, then you can present yourself as a team player that knows how to motivate others. If a company is undergoing a big shift in operations and you have experience teaching new systems to people on a sports team, then point out this connection in the interview. Basically think about *your* mission statement and the company's. How do these two missions work together? Weave your core assets, skills, traits, and experience into the tapestry of the company. Analyze for yourself why you are the right person right now.

3. Dress for Success

This may sound like a no-brainer, but it's important that you present yourself as a neat, well put-together person who will represent the company in a professional manner. If possible, find out ahead of time whether the company's attire is formal, business casual, or some other attire. Often you can get a sense of how to dress by visiting the company's website and finding a picture of your prospective interviewer. One candidate did this prior to an interview with the dean of a prominent MBA program. To her surprise, she found that the dean of the business school dressed informally in the brochure as well as in other pictures on the website. She decided to dress in a less formal suit so as to look professional and serious about her interest in the position without looking too rigid.

You should do your homework in order to dress appropriately for the office you are seeking to join. If you must err, err on the side of being a little overdressed. The most important goal is to give off your most charismatic vibe. However, be careful to keep that vibe business-like. Don't display any piercings. Remove all facial jewelry, with the exception of appropriate, modest earrings. Cover all visible tattoos. Some interviewers talk in terms of the "beer test." Passing the beer test is fairly simple: just be someone that co-workers would like to go out and grab a beer with. If you pass this test then you may be a more viable candidate for the job. Although you're being hired to do a job, not to make friends, never underestimate the power of image and likability.

Start at your head and work your way down to make sure you're ready for the interview. Your hair should be neat and clean. Ladies, avoid distracting hair accessories and don't make the mistake of wearing a hat. Also keep the make-up light. Nobody wants to hire a clown except the circus. Gentlemen, try a nice, clean-shaven look. Make sure your breath doesn't smell bad. It was a turn-off in high school, and it's a turn-off now. Don't eat an onion or garlic bagel for breakfast. Poppy seed muffins are probably a mistake as well as they can leave tiny black seeds stuck in your teeth. Oral hygiene is just as important as overall hygiene.

Once you have your head on straight, begin to focus on the rest of your body. Select your clothes the night before. Check for holes, loose hems, loose buttons, and stains. Iron your outfit or have it dry-cleaned. Ladies, we recommend taking an extra pair of pantyhose with you in case of emergencies. Make sure your nails are trimmed nicely as you will be shaking a lot of hands. You should also avoid wild and crazy colors of nail polish in favor of neutral colors.

Far from being superficial, these tips are all about helping you to appear professional and present the best image. You want your interviewer(s) to remember your attributes and how you can add value to the firm. Why gain strikes against you for careless wardrobe malfunctions?

4. The First Moments are Critical

As you already know, the first ten minutes are crucial. It's a good idea to do a *dry run* to the destination the day before at around the same time as the scheduled interview. Get a handle on the logistics of parking and where the office is. Find out your route as well as any road construction and traffic patterns so that you won't be late. *You must never be late to any interview!* By taking care of these logistics beforehand, you will be more relaxed and thus make a more positive first impression.

We also recommend never accepting a beverage of any kind. If there is even a one percent chance that you might spill the drink, just forget about it and politely decline. Always smile and be courteous to *everyone* you come into contact with: the doorman, receptionist, interns, everyone. They all have opinions that may be heard, and they might be more highly valued than you realize. You don't want them telling the boss that you seemed self-centered or smug; you never know where a gatekeeper may lurk.

We know of one instance where a very viable candidate marched into a law office and completely offended the receptionist and the hiring partner's secretary with a poor attitude. The two office workers commented that "the kid was a real jerk," and he was not hired. The law partner emphasized, "Even though he seemed almost perfect for the position, no one would have wanted to work with him or for him."

5. Communicate Your Message

Before answering a question, always give yourself a few moments to think about your answer, even if you have already prepared it. This will help you settle yourself and communicate more effectively. Keep in mind that you can tailor your answer to virtually any question to point out positive facts about you and your character traits. For example, one candidate was asked whether she could think on her feet. She told the interviewer of an anecdote involving a conference where a key speaker cancelled at the last minute. Instead of panicking, she called a professor who had done work in the field, and they came up with a short program to replace the speaker. The interviewer was intrigued and charmed, and the candidate got the job. The point is to be able to back up any claim that you make with a good, tangible example. How can you claim that you're good under pressure if this interview is making you sweat?

Also, don't bore the interviewer with unnecessary details. Your answers are advertisements for *your* brand. Be interesting and give smart, concise, and thoughtful answers. Wrap your experiences in a nice, marketable package, and don't discount your own credibility.

You might be surprised how your past, seemingly menial, jobs can be used effectively in interviews. One candidate for an international bank won over the board with his tales of being a "garbage man" one summer. Another interviewee won a spot at a top law firm by detailing her work at a busy children's store juggling screaming toddlers, demanding mothers, and a mountain of inventory paperwork. The key is that this interviewee translated her work experience into desirable skills—the ability to multitask and stay focused under pressure. Ask yourself: What experiences and skills can I use to demonstrate that I'd be the perfect candidate for this particular position?

Another example of making such an impression can be seen in the story of a student who was committed to environmentalism. She witnessed hundreds of useful items being thrown out of the dorms at the end of each semester. She coordinated the efforts of the student government, the Pan-Hellenic council, and the administration. Now a "donate, don't dump" campaign lives on at her university. This innovative program won her a position at a very exciting nonprofit organization.

6. Demonstrate Your Skill Set

As we have indicated, this is a very important aspect of interviewing. You must communicate the mantra "If it matters to you, then it matters to me" when responding to questions. You want to market yourself as a person who is able to listen, be flexible and accommodating, and who will work with others in an environment of sincerity and mutual helpfulness. To do this, you have to point to situations when you have demonstrated these qualities.

For example, one student volunteered once a week at a local organization to help children with special needs. This student became so passionate and engaged in her work there that she encouraged dozens of her classmates to join her each week. This experience demonstrates her skill in being an influencer, an initiator, and a powerful recruiter. Again, the emphasis here is to show that you have the assets and skills to add value to the company.

Another student suffered debilitating injuries that kept him on the sidelines of his college basketball team. After multiple surgeries and rehabilitation, he fought his way back to the starting lineup, and the team rallied around him to win a championship. This student could use this situation to enforce his skills in leadership, commitment, and determination.

Discuss situations where you have used your passion to influence others to follow your lead. Have you used your strong reasoning and analysis to entice your peers? Are there situations where you have shown your ability to "stick with it?" Such examples of your tenacity will serve you well in an interview. Begin to build a repertoire of experiences that you can share in an interview to back your claim that your abilities will meet the needs of the company.

7. Practice, Practice, Practice

This step is probably the most difficult to master, but like anything, it just takes practice. You can practice your communicative skills by yourself, with friends and family, with career coaches, with career service centers (which often offer mock interview sessions), or even with your goldfish. On top of the suggestions we made about how to behave during an interview, you also should be aware of your surroundings. Use the office to gather information about the interviewer. You can be a modern-day Sherlock Holmes and carefully dissect the office with your eyes! Are there diplomas on the wall? Where are they from? What about pictures of family on the desk? Vacation photos from places your interviewer has traveled?

You want to use this information to find out what you can about this person. Use your environment to also point out your own character traits that you think the interviewer may be interested in. For example, if you know that the job might involve some travel, and you see a vacation photo on the interviewer's desk, you could remark, "Oh, is that a photo from Hawaii? I went there on a vacation last summer. I really love to travel." Your love for travel may then be transferred to your willingness to travel for work if necessary. In this way, you're not just creating rapport with the interviewer; you're also demonstrating your *social intelligence* in tying experiences into character traits.

One successful interviewee noticed several photos from foot races and that her interviewer wore a sophisticated sports watch. The job candidate mentioned her love of running charity races, and the two shared an instant connection. A marathon runner may show endurance, the ability to "break through" seemingly insurmountable walls, training, discipline, and mental strength, not to mention the fact that a common interest is often a solid foundation for a good relationship. Do not underestimate the power of being an athlete—and the appreciation and respect you will receive from other athletes. Whether you have a particular strength in athletics, music, art, theater, etc. or whether you love pets, travel, or building model airplanes, etc., the idea is to find common ground with the interviewer or to show how this particular interest or passion will fuel your ability to be a great candidate for this job.

Another candidate came from a large family and noticed a family photo in the office of the interviewer that also displayed a very large family. The "lessons learned" from a large family became the focus of the successful interview. These lessons included frugality, accommodation, sharing, and negotiation, the ability to work in a small personal space, compromise, and persuasiveness with a particular agenda. This candidate found a lot of common ground with this interviewer!

8. The Old Maxims Still Ring True

Much of the old wisdom that was endlessly imparted upon your parents and grandparents applies today. You should communicate to the interviewer that you are willing to put in the hours and **pay your dues** in terms of hard work for the company. Make it clear that you aren't looking for an instant career—you are going to put the time in to build what will be, if hired, a long, mutually productive relationship.

Use your years of dedication to your education as one indicator of your ability to stick to a goal. Indicate your eagerness to do whatever it takes to get the job done. Being a *Johnny or Jane on the spot* is also an important quality to have. You must be willing to go beyond the call of duty.

Finally, *follow the leader* is an important concept for most companies. Although interviewers look for leadership qualities that prove a person can do independent work, ultimately they are looking for employees that can follow orders and do what they are told without causing a fuss. Be compliant, not complacent.

9. Have Great Questions to Ask the Interviewer

There will come a time in most interviews when the interviewer will ask, "So do you have any questions for me?" *Don't be caught off guard and say you don't have any questions.* Research and formulate questions before the interview. Don't choose questions about things like benefits and salary. Ask questions that present meaningful insights into the particular job you're applying for. This is one of the best opportunities to show the interviewer that you are interested in the company and have done your homework.

At this point, it would be advisable to say, "I was looking through the prospectus and mission statement of the company, and I have some sense of the corporate culture, though perhaps you could share a little more with me?" By corporate culture, you are asking what it's like to work for the company. For example, companies such as Ben & Jerry's and Zappos are both known to boast fairly informal working environments. Casual dress is the norm. Allegedly, at Zappos, there is no division between spaces for higher-authority figures (upper management) and people in the sales division. The message here is that everyone's contribution is of equal value. If such a liberal working environment is important to you, then make sure of its existence before taking a job. Are there small tasks or technical skill sets required for new hires? Do only the partners have the leadership roles? What are the intangibles? By asking these questions and more, you're suggesting that you think the general atmosphere seems so great that you'd like to learn even more about it. You might even say something to the effect of, "I can see myself thriving in this type of environment and there's great alignment with my skill sets. Can you tell me more about this?"

Use their answers as a springboard to go even more in depth with your inquiries about the position and company. Your questions should always subtly communicate your interest, ability, and compatibility with the position as well.

10. Interviewing: How to Answer the Question "What Is Your Biggest Weakness?"

Never initiate the conversation of discussing your weaknesses. However, in the event the interviewer poses this question, consider what he or she is really trying to assess. Are you able to admit you're wrong? Can you turn a situation around? Are you willing to change when you make a mistake?

The way that you answer this question will allow you to demonstrate your emotional maturity and humility. Are you able to admit that you make mistakes? Are you obstinately sure that you are always right? Do you recognize that you are a good leader, but that there is give and take involved in any leadership position?

One point mentioned by hundreds of interviewers is that while you should not shoot yourself in the foot by admitting a huge weakness that will conflict with this particular job, you should be able to answer the question, highlighting a situation where you fell short of the mark. You should also try to show how you learned from the mistake.

Our advice is to pre-think this question thoroughly for each job interview. It's one of the toughest you'll face. Don't resort to the indulgent, "Oh, my biggest weakness is that I'm a perfectionist" or "I always give 200 percent to every job I undertake." The interviewer will sense the brown-nosing insincerity of these responses. However, you should be able to highlight the "take away" message of your weakness—specifically what you have learned and how you are turning this negative into a positive.

One job candidate interviewed with a team of international bankers. He responded to the "weakness" question by discussing deadlines. "I'm usually a calm team player. However, when faced with a deadline I often get angry when others aren't doing their part to meet the deadline. I usually choose to get the project completed and then apologize later for any excessive anger." After recalling his earlier conversations with some of the interviewers, who all played a lot of recreational basketball, the candidate added, "My jump shot could use some work too." The interviewers all smiled and he got the job.

Another student interviewing for a legal clerkship met with partners of a law firm. She admitted that her weakness occurs when she "gets on a roll" with her work and becomes so immersed in the project that she often forgets to save documents. Twice while working last year, she lost her work to power outages and a computer crash. "I learned my lesson," she stated. "Now I post a huge note next to my workspace that states 'Save.' I have a permanent post-it note on my laptop that gives me the same message. I haven't made that mistake again!" The interviewer smiled at the student's honesty and willingness to take steps to "take away" a lesson. She got the job.

TO SUM IT UP:

- Don't volunteer a weakness.
- Don't communicate a weakness pertinent for performing this job well.
- Mention a weakness but explain how you learned from the situation.
- Be authentic and show the best sides of your personality.

Remember: Don't emphasize or dwell on your weaknesses. Focus on the learning experiences they gave you and your ability to rebound from your mistakes.

Lastly, keep your private life and private thoughts as private as possible. We second the motion to carefully safeguard the impression that your Facebook, Blogs, or Tweets may give others. Use your time with an interviewer to showcase your positive qualities: your accountability, your outgoing nature, your willingness to take on more than your share, and your desire to positively influence your environment. Your "pros" should always outweigh your "cons" so that you leave the interviewer wowed and positive about hiring you.

ONE LAST NOTE ABOUT PURSUING YOUR FIRST CAREER OPPORTUNITY:

Here are a few tips to keep in mind as you launch your first career. Some of these points have been elaborated on in this chapter, but all of them merit being mentioned here as they are very important in affecting how potential employers perceive you.

1. **Let everyone you know hear about your job search**—your network should extend to family, friends, teachers, former co-workers, former employers, and online networking sites.

2. **Proofread every document you write.**

3. **Do your homework.** Personalize cover letters with the NAME of the hiring manager.

4. **Don't act casual if you aspire to be a professional.** Be clear and not cute in all conversations and e-mails.

5. **Don't utilize the same resume for every position.** A little homework will go a long way.

6. **Preserve your online image, making sure that any posting of you is appropriate and unquestionable.**

7. **Mind your manners**—express your appreciation to every person you encounter along the way, whether or not their efforts on your behalf are helpful or not. Try to send a thank you note to every hiring manager you meet.

STEP 5:

Construct Success With Your Research and Toolbox

Throughout this book, we have been encouraging and showing you to make solid, informed decisions about your career path. We hope that in perusing this guide, you have learned a lot about locating a suitable industry, finding a great place to live, networking with professionals, nailing that interview, and so much more. Now it's time to take this knowledge and put it to good use.

NEEDS ANALYSIS, STUDY YOURSELF:

The ultimate message of this book is: study yourself. People spend thousands of dollars and countless hours with career counselors, with one ultimate goal: to discover and identify strengths, weaknesses, passions, interests, core values, and establish goals for the future. When used properly, the tools in this book will be your road map on the journey to the aforementioned discoveries. Use this collated information to maximize your potential and expedite the process of self-discovery as it relates to finding the right career, getting hired, and having a happy life. If you take the time now to reflect and learn about yourself through introspection, you will avoid much heartache later. You want your employment to be comparable to a long-term relationship as opposed to a summer fling. In order to truly enter into matrimonial career bliss, you must be able to analyze your needs, interests, strengths, values, and passions. Every decision you make in your journey should relate back to these points. This is your personal mission statement. You should strive to keep this analysis as a blueprint to help you decide where to work, whom to work for, and your work/family balance.

Don't take any short cuts in thinking through all these areas. You need to develop a theory to govern your life. Of course, you will evolve and change, so your needs, interests, strengths, values, and passions will evolve and change as well. Our advice to you is to make each decision based on this set of criteria. Your journey must be right for *you*. The chart below will help you set your compass.

Knowing more about your needs and wants will point you in the right direction. Oftentimes a chart can be used to flesh out these needs. Many visual thinkers find benefit from charts. The chart below can help you visualize what is important to you. Just be honest about what you really want out of life and what your interests and abilities are.

INTERESTS... Activities that give you Pleasure	PASSIONS... Where you want to make a difference

STRENGTHS...	DESIRED AREAS FOR GROWTH...
Areas where you excel and your record of achievement	Skills and traits you can improve upon

Also consider questions such as the following:
- Are you a "people person?"
- Are you good with numbers?
- Do you prefer working indoors or outdoors?
- Do you like crowds or isolation?
- Do you need direction and supervision?
- Are you thorough and detailed or creative and big-picture minded?
- Do you want to balance a career with family?
- Do you like to travel?
- Do you need financial independence?
- How important is job security or job risk?
- How open are you to change?

Once you have analyzed your personal needs and desires, look at the needs of society. How can your needs in the chart above match the needs of society or with the businesses and industries of society? By doing this analysis, you will begin to see where you fit in—where your skills will be useful. If you are doing something that you love and for which you have an aptitude, and you are contributing to a greater good, then you have the two main ingredients for the recipe of success.

YOU CAN DO IT!

Don't give up. If your first interview is a catastrophe (or even if it goes well but you still don't get the job) take the time to reflect on what you learned from the experience. Every interview is an opportunity to learn how to relate better with interviewers. Every interview can be looked at as preparation for another interview. So look at your failures as an opportunity to learn and succeed later. Always stay positive and have confidence in yourself.

When faced with a seemingly insurmountable challenge, there are two ways in which people typically respond. They either give up and accept defeat or they bounce back, fight even harder, and are determined to grow through their challenges. In addition to being able to handle your failures with grace, you need to develop resilience, perseverance, and endurance. Expect to be faced with rejection, disappointment, and other setbacks. Take your ego out of the equation in order to look at yourself objectively and honestly. The strength of your character will not be measured by your ability to dodge failure but rather by your ability to rebound and grow from it.

LEARN TO LOVE CRITICISM:

Although your grandmother may see you as "the perfect angel," the rest of the world knows that no one is perfect—not even you. It is time to face the facts: everyone is flawed, and most people will receive more criticism than positive reinforcement in their careers, social lives, home lives, and everywhere else. So what message can we take from criticism? Is there a positive message at all?

While the title of this section may have caused your eyes to pop out of your skull, please understand that we are referring to *constructive criticism*. Understand that before you are able to make use of constructive criticism, you must know your strengths and be confident in your abilities. A sense of humor is also crucial. Trust us—once you grow enough to become immune to vulnerability, you will realize that criticism is your greatest gift. In fact, you should feel nothing but gratitude for those who criticize you, even if those criticisms come in a seemingly offensive package.

If the criticism does seem overly harsh, just be sure to take it with a grain of salt—but don't ignore it all together. Even if you do not agree with the criticism you are given, there is usually some *kernel of truth* in it that will help you to reach your potential. You know your strengths and weaknesses. Use peoples' criticism of you or your work as means to hammer out your personal kinks. When people point out your limitations, make every effort to keep your ego in check and not take the suggestion personally. By turning the tables on criticism and using it to your advantage, you will be able to learn from your mistakes at a formidable rate. Leave your ego at the door. Realize that true self-confidence comes from being able to know your strengths and not feel vulnerable or backed into a corner when someone points out your weaknesses.

Think of criticism as free career advice. Sometimes criticism stings at first. After all, no one likes to hear negativity, no matter how well the intentions are. However, you should try to let the sting pass over you like a cloud, and don't become paralyzed by the initial blow. You can't control what others say, but you can control how you react to them.

Being able to take criticism is a character trait much sought after in the business world. Managers and hiring specialists don't want to work with people who get defensive whenever they're given criticism. Nor do companies want to hire individuals who are content with mediocrity. A person who can take criticism, reflect on it, and then use it to strengthen his or her skills is highly attractive to any interviewer or employer.

Self-esteem is not thinking you're the best at everything and know everything. That's called narcissism. Real self-esteem comes from knowing your strengths and limitations and then always working toward becoming a more complete person: a more effective worker, a more supportive spouse, a more reliable friend, a more amicable co-worker, etc.

CHARTING A COURSE:

So now that you've read this timely guide, what's the next step? Simply this: plan out your future. Don't take short cuts. Do the research and take time to reflect on what will truly make you happy. You must pay your dues now. This is the time in your life when you are most able to make the sacrifices that will help you get to the top of your game. Add to your value by looking for opportunities to be helpful. Come early, stay late, and ask for more work (if you can) to stand apart from the rest of the crowd. Anyone at least a decade older than you will be able to tell you that, in hindsight, their extra work and their sacrifices paid off. You are charting a course for your life and we want to be your constant companion, so remember that you can always come back to this guide.

IMPORTANT POINTS TO REMEMBER AS YOU START YOUR JOURNEY INTO YOUR FUTURE:

- Use this book as a "mentor" to project out ten years from now what will make you happy.
- When applying to college or graduate school, reinforce what value you can add to the school. Remember: schools are run like businesses. They want to invest wisely.
- Research the industry and companies you're interested in. Most importantly, identify their needs.
- When you meet the needs of a company, it will ultimately meet your needs through promotions and salary increases.
- Always be neat, clean, and well dressed at your interviews.
- Choose your city first, then your job; your long-term happiness depends very much on where you live.
- Find the *kernel of truth* within any criticism and use it as a means of self-improvement.

For Girls' Eyes Only – Special Considerations for Young Women in Today's Economy

Today's working woman embraces a culture of flexibility, oftentimes juggling dual roles as both a "career woman" and a "family woman." For most young women, the future holds some hybrid of entering a working world and starting a family. As companies become more sensitive to the various demands placed on women who want both a career and a family, many changes are taking place in the job market. Personal relationships and familial roles are changing as well. Although some couples do share family responsibilities and some men even take the dominant role in family care and housework, these responsibilities still usually fall on the shoulders of the woman, whether she has a career or not. This chapter will help guide you in preparing for this life of dual roles—career woman and family woman—and how to succeed in both.

According to a 2009 employee benefits survey from *Working Mother* magazine, 54 percent of the nation's employers offer some sort of flexible working arrangement and almost half offer a telecommuting option. Other lifestyle benefits are also increasingly popular in today's workplace. These statistics indicate an important message: *Do your research.* Whether you're going straight into the workforce from undergraduate school or seeking your first post-graduate position, you need to figure out which companies and firms are making it possible to be a working mother and where these companies are located.

Even women graduates of the most prestigious and selective universities have plans of combining career with family at some point. A few years ago, a famous study focused on a graduating class of Yale University reported that 60 percent of women in this elite school planned to cut back on work or stop working entirely to have and raise children. Even with these astonishing numbers, only a few schools are establishing programs to prepare women to "step-out" and then to "re-enter" the workforce after spending time home with children. Hopefully the myriad of programs, workshops, recruiting firms, coaches, and consultants will grow exponentially as people everywhere work to assist women with the competing demands of work and family.

The problem is that many jobs are organized around a full standard work week, and challenging these arrangements can be difficult. For the most part, women must broker flexible working arrangements using exceptional credentials or skills. On the plus side, flexible workers may be available at more affordable rates, and therefore nonprofit groups, small businesses, and start-up companies may be eager to make a deal and be more flexible with scheduling.

The goal is to find a business solution for stay-at-home mothers who don't want to make a once-in-a-lifetime decision between working and staying at home. There are several ways of handling the conflict: take a brief hiatus from work, use some combination of flextime and reduced hours while home hours are in demand, or move to a part-time work situation. As a solution, part-time work is often a drawback in most professional work settings. Many part-time jobs pay little and don't provide benefits. One research center found that approximately two-thirds of women who leave work to raise children want to re-enter professional life but feel that companies are reluctant to hire them. In fact, one study reports that female professionals who take three or more years off earn 37 percent less, on average, than women who don't take time off.

What is a woman to do?

Well, it begins with preparing now for what is probably inevitable: at some point, you may wish to have a family. If this is the case, you must position yourself as best you can to fulfill all of your goals. That means you should carefully examine your choice of college, graduate school, career, and city. You should gather information from women who have been down the path before, and learn from their experiences. The following is a list of specific programs at top universities that currently assist women in this process; pay close attention as other schools are certain to soon follow suit.

HOW HIGHER EDUCATION IS FOCUSING ON WOMEN'S CAREER NEEDS:

Harvard Business School (HBS) introduced a program called "Charting Your Course," where alumnae were invited to come to HBS for two days to develop a strategic plan to return to work. One group included women who were stepping out for a few years to raise children and wanted a strategy to bridge the gap, keep skills current, and keep networks going. Another group of women were ready to return to the workforce but needed the tools to re-enter the market, to find the right employers, and to negotiate flexible working conditions. HBS also offered a more intense program called "New Path," a six-day immersion to help women ascertain how their particular field had changed during their absence, how finance and information technologies have advanced, and how new tools could be utilized to make contact with prospective employers.

A few other elite schools have been developing similar programs to help women either rejoin the workforce after a break or to manage some combination of career and family work. Dartmouth's Tuck School of Business launched a "Back in Business" program to address the needs of women returning to work after taking time off to raise kids. Pepperdine University is at the forefront of these efforts, offering a part-time MBA program specifically designed for stay-at-home moms. Stanford's Graduate School of Business is addressing the problem with several executive education programs for moms. Babson College offers a variety of programs through the Center for Women's Leadership, through education, outreach, and research that assist women in achieving leadership goals. They also assist women in areas from stepping back into the workforce to global women's entrepreneurship. Columbia University's "Mothers in Business" is one of the nation's first organized groups that specifically addresses the concerns of MBA moms. The group offers roundtable discussions with alumni and provides networking opportunities and support services for women with children.

Another innovative program is at the Wharton School of Business at the University of Pennsylvania. Monica McGrath, Wharton adjunct professor of management, has studied the difficulties women face upon their return to the labor force and co-authored a study called "Back in the Game, Returning to Business after a Hiatus: Experience and Recommendations for Women, Employers, and Universities." *According to McGrath, women should prepare for their return to work from the moment they leave.* She suggests staying up-to-date on skills and keeping a hand in the working world while on hiatus. *This may include keeping up professional licenses, taking courses, and staying connected with professional contacts, even if done informally.* McGrath poses short-term consulting jobs or project work as viable options. Women can also improve their chances of job re-entry by keeping up with technology changes while out of the workforce.

McGrath suggests that a woman state her case for hiring unapologetically and proactively, framing her story in business terms and with a positive tone. For example, "I felt I could make a better impact with my children by staying home for these years, and this is how I have stayed current with my skills." Work for a parent/teacher organization could be framed as, "I was part of a team that raised over $100,000 in a fundraising effort." McGrath urges schools to offer targeted career services, alumni networks, and educational programs for women hoping to eventually re-enter the workforce, and she urges students to ascertain various career path options that they may want to take after they have worked a few years. According to McGrath, "We need to encourage women to think of their career as a lifetime. They need to be asked, 'What's your game plan?' Companies are diligent and strategic in planning the path for a talented person's career. As women, we need to do a better job of that ourselves."

CAREER COACHING FOR RE-ENTRY WOMEN:

A myriad of businesses are popping up throughout the country to assist women with re-entry scenarios and in managing the home/work balance with flextime and other options. These firms assist professional women in finding part-time or flexible jobs and include coaches and consultants who help women hone their resumes and track down alternative jobs that will make use of their education and experience. Some private companies include:

- Quest for Balance in Seattle
- Flexperience in San Francisco
- Flex-Time Lawyers in New York and Philadelphia
- iRelaunch in New Jersey and Boston
- 10 Til 2 in Denver and other cities
- Round Peg Group in Alexandria, Virginia
- Mom Corps based in Atlanta but offering offices in several other cities, including Bethesda, Maryland.
- Aquent Marketing Staffing, the world's largest staffing firm for marketing professionals, is working with leading business schools and career counselors to help women find flexible work options including "temp-to-perm" situations, full-time and part-time interim projects, and work-from-home interim projects. Aquent Marketing Staffing is a division of global professional services firm Aquent (Aquent.com). Headquartered in Boston, Aquent has a network of more than sixty offices in sixteen countries.

PLANNING TO "HAVE IT ALL" BEGINS NOW – SEVEN STRATEGIES TO HELP:

If you are planning to balance career and family responsibilities at some point in the future, your preparation for that goal must begin now. The following seven strategies will help you make strong decisions now that will aid in your ability to make the most of your education and work experience without sacrificing the choice to raise a family.

1. Investigate All of Your Options in Your Chosen Field of Study

Don't feel as if you have to pick the most grueling, seemingly glamorous career in your field of interest. Remember, you may be stepping out for a while to raise a family. If you are considering law, medicine, or business, have you investigated which fields are easiest for re-entry, for remaining up-to-date and current, or for flexible working situations? Is the position you're pursuing capable of absorbing time off for maternity or family leave? Ask yourself whether you want the responsibilities of becoming a full-fledged partner in a firm or whether your personal goals may be met with a less demanding position. Seek out a woman who has done these things and ask her how she managed, what obstacles she encountered, and what she might have done differently.

Once you've assembled some information from real life sources, ask yourself the tough questions such as: "Will I be happy as a nurse or a physician's assistant or do I truly want to be a doctor?" or "Do I really want to be on partner track in a high-profile litigation firm or will I be happy as a part-time attorney in a thriving tax or patent law firm?"

The bottom line is to think about what you really want, seek out help from others who have already been there, and be sure to consider *all* the options in your field.

2. Have a Plan For Balancing Your Relationship With Your Spouse

If you want to be the main breadwinner and you want a family, then be aware of the dynamic you're setting up for yourself. If your main goal is to show your significant other how capable you are and how you have the drive to be a full-time, high-powered career woman then be prepared for him to assume you mean it! When you add a family to the mix, know that you will probably be the one wearing two hats for the big portion of every day. It's therefore important to plan with your spouse how best to balance your work life with your family life.

3. Find a Mentor

As with every career search, the more you learn from others, the less chance you have of making avoidable mistakes. Remember that it's always more difficult to learn things the hard way. Career women should ask themselves, "How will I manage my life?" To learn how, find a person who has carved out a position utilizing flextime principles and someone who has a fulfilling job in her area of interest but is working only part-time. You may learn of less demanding opportunities within a particular field that will suit you as you raise a family. Of course, each woman has particular skills and a unique partnership and home situation. For example, some spouses are extremely involved in home/ child care; others are definitely not! Many are somewhere in between—they try to help but don't assume the bulk of the responsibility. You must, in the end, evaluate for yourself what will work best for you. Do so with the aid of the experience of someone who has travelled this road before.

4. Stay Involved Through Networking and Education

Even if you take time off to have a child or stay home with children, you should always prepare for the day when you may re-enter the workforce. Therefore be your own best friend and *keep connected.* In this economy, networking is the number one learning experience that people in career transition have gained. Networking should be considered a way of life, according to leadership coaching specialist Regina Oblinsky. She defines networking as twofold. "It's relationship building and knowledge building if you think of it in those terms, then you need to continue the process throughout your career in some capacity." When you think of networking, Oblinsky suggests doing it in a "give first" perspective. Think along the lines of best practices, she explains. There might be something you did in a former company or information that you gleaned through your job search activities that you can incorporate into your new role. Here are some additional practical ways to stay involved although there are many more depending on what field you're in:

- Stay in touch with key players in your industry
- Go to local and regional meetings of like-minded professionals

- Subscribe to publications in your field to stay up-to-date
- Seek additional certifications and continuing education credits

Whatever it takes, stay current. And don't forget to update your resume! For example, if you're in market research and become proficient using Oracle, JMP, SAS, Omniture, and/or Webtrends, then make note of this on your resume. We strongly suggest that you become a specialist of some sort in order to stay viable in a particular area of your field. This time investment now will pay off later once the kids are grown up and you want to move back into a career. In fact, these ideas are important to consider even when you select a graduate program. Ask if your business school or law school has any particular programs to help you upon re-entry.

Don't fall out of touch with the personal network of professionals you've formed over the years. Continue to make contacts at social events and professional meetings that you attend while raising a family. This will take a specific effort on your part, especially if you have toddlers running around the house. It's well worth it in the long run. Think about taking the time every few months to connect with your network by sending an e-mail, an invitation for coffee, or a holiday card. Don't overlook other moms who have professional and social networks of their own that could be quite useful to you.

5. Consider a Career Re-Invention

Many women find that their life experiences, skills, and connections support venturing out into another field or specialized area when they step back into the job market. For example, one woman moved from working with non-profit organizations to a career as a corporate grant writer. Another woman moved from being an event planner to working as an event coordinator for a lobbyist group. A research biochemist could switch to organizing drug testing for pharmaceutical companies. One clinical toxicologist left her job at a medical center, enrolled in a wine class, found internships, and is a winemaker in Napa Valley! The point is very similar to the first one: consider all of your options. Talk to someone who does what you find interesting and rewarding. Use your time off to explore new interests through books, workshops, and even sessions with a qualified career coach. Don't be afraid to make a change. Take an organized approach to research and prepare to pursue your best options.

6. Do Some Work from Home

Showcase your telecommuting-friendly skills such as writing, research, and proofreading, and find work creating marketing materials, conducting resume screening, making preliminary telephone interviews, or other project work. You can look into editing other authors' texts or writing your own how-to articles on websites such as BrightHub.com and eHow.com. There's a lot of freelance work out there that can provide substantial supplemental income from the convenience of your office chair. Job boards are often a resource for finding freelance work in many areas and disciplines. Check out some of the following:

- www.jobsandmoms.com
- www.teleworkrecruiting.com

- www.tjobs.com
- www.aquent.us
- www.cybertemp.com
- www.elance.com.
- www.eworkexchange.com
- www.guru.com
- www.hireability.com
- www.workaholicsforHire.com

7. Strategically Volunteer

If you are faced with requests for volunteer work, especially with school-age children, strategically choose assignments that will either teach you new skills or help you in meeting your future career goals. For example, look for leadership positions, fundraising opportunities, writing or graphic design needs, or management of events. All of these volunteer opportunities translate very well into business skills and experience. Be sure to keep an accurate and complete log of all you do so that you can showcase these skills later.

THE FAMILY/CAREER DECISION – REAL LIFE STORIES TO HELP YOU CHART YOUR COURSE:

We have interviewed many women on their decisions to raise a family and journey through the working world, and the results of those interviews are as diverse as the women themselves. Women, of course, come in every size, shape, and socio-economic background, and that diversity does not end when it comes to the broad range of preferences regarding the focus on family and careers. Your experience will be different than your mother's, your sister's, your mentor's. There is no way we can address the specifics of each woman's situation in this chapter, but we do offer several real-life stories of women that convey a broad spectrum of experience. We hope that when you read about these women, you may find some common ground that will help you plan your future.

Each story, including your own, is unique. Whether you decide to wait to have a family or wait to pursue a full-time career, the decision is not always clear. Some women don't have the luxury of even making the decision; they don't have an option financially. Most women don't fall distinctly into one single category, and most women lead dynamic lives where the balance shifts from time to time. We speak in general terms about a "general focus," though we fully understand that this focus often shifts. We hope you find these stories both helpful and inspirational.

We have loosely grouped these stories into three categories: women who have focused on family early, delaying a career; women who have focused on career first, delaying or foregoing an early family life; women who have combined career and family, sometimes switching career paths to accommodate the demands of their families. After the following stories, we summarize the "pros and cons" of focusing early on family and focusing early on career, as well as attempting to balance family and career from the beginning of the journey. Please note that all names have been changed to protect privacy.

EARLY FAMILY FOCUS, DELAYED CAREER:

Reva

Reva obtained a graduate degree in music from Wayne State University. Her career goals were to become a pre-school teacher and a part-time piano teacher working from home. She married her college sweetheart, a swimmer on the university swim team. He became a physician and she stayed home to raise their three children and taught piano part-time from her home. When her husband was diagnosed with a debilitating disease at age 30, Reva was forced to find work. The family did not have disability insurance. Reva began to sell cosmetics and silk flowers from home while she earned a license to sell real estate and insurance. Within years, she became the leading insurance sales person in her state. Now, at 77, she still works full time. Her children and grandchildren marvel at her resilience and perseverance. She kicked and screamed at having to enter the workforce but remains thrilled with her career and family success.

Mandy

Mandy, a pediatrician, worked for two years in private practice on Long Island. Her husband commuted each morning to Wall Street. With the birth of her first child, Mandy ceased practicing medicine. The couple had four children, each eighteen months apart. When Mandy tried to return to her career, the family was in distress. She could not find adequate childcare, and no one was interested in hiring her on an extreme part-time basis. Mandy made a decision: the family would return to her hometown in Ohio, where her parents and sisters could help with childcare. Her husband would remain in New York during the work week and would commute to Ohio from Thursday to Sunday. As the children became school aged, Mandy found a job one weekend a month at a pediatric emergency clinic. With the help of her family, and her husband's help on weekends, Mandy has been able to ease back into her career. She expressed, "Although the arrangement was unconventional, it worked!"

McKenzie

McKenzie, an attorney from a prestigious Midwestern law school, left the practice of law after working as a clerk in federal court and as a litigator for a small boutique firm. When pregnant with her first child, McKenzie left the practice of law. Her husband, a car dealer, worked long hours, and the couple did not have family nearby. When her four children became school age, McKenzie tried to find a job in the legal field. Twelve years out, there was not a law firm interested in her outdated resume! McKenzie began to use her research and writing skills, assisting corporations with freelance writing projects and students with research and writing projects. She started her own business, using the contacts she had made through her children's schools. She now owns a thriving tutoring service, which grows larger as each of her children leaves the nest for college. Although not as lucrative as a legal career, the tutoring career provides flexibility and self-satisfaction. She loves her new work, but she regrets not staying current with a particular area of specialization in the law. She would advise young female attorneys to remain involved in a particular legal

area through networking and continuing legal education—
if they are interested in a career in the law after children!

Michelle

Michelle graduated from an Ivy League school and attended a top medical school. She began her career as an
emergency room doctor and a newlywed. After two years
of working in an urban hospital, she learned that she was
expecting her first child. She made the decision to place her
medical career on hold for the first year of the child's life.
Twenty years and three children later, Michelle gloried in
her decision to stay home. Her husband, the primary breadwinner, worked long hours to support their young family.

Michelle continued to receive the leading journals in
emergency medicine. Several times a year, she volunteered
to teach CPR classes at community outreach programs. As
her children grew older, she offered her services in the
nurse's office at school and at summer camps. Far from miss-
ing her medical practice, she enjoyed each stage of motherhood. Because she stayed current with medical practices,
attending seminars and online lectures, she found gratify-
ing and well-paying part-time work at an emergency clinic.
Michelle has no regrets and has happily stayed home, a
full-time mom for most of her children's lives.

Lauren

Lauren was a merchandiser for a large food conglom-
erate. She left the working world after ten years to raise
her two sons. Her husband, a corporate attorney, worked
his way to a well-paying position that allowed Lauren to
stay home with her sons. She had been a rising star at her

company. While home for ten years, she continued to network and utilized her marketing skills to raise thousands of dollars for her kids' private school. She stayed involved in civic groups and attended monthly meetings of professionals in her field. Eventually she re-entered the workforce with a local advertising agency, starting as an independent contractor working on specific campaigns and events. She has just been offered a full-time position, doing exactly what she did before staying home.

FULL-TIME CAREER FOCUS, DELAYING OR NOT HAVING CHILDREN:

Sandy

Sandy is the vice president of a thriving Midwestern bank. She started in the bank at a low-paying job and worked her way up the corporate ladder. She has never married and doesn't have children. She is very involved in community activities. Although she doesn't have a spouse, she isn't lonely. She's a happy, successful career woman. She lives in an area of town dense with businesspeople that like to socialize, with a lovely social club nearby where she dines, exercises, and swims. She has moved around quite a bit throughout her career, and being single without a family has worked to her business advantage in many ways.

Susan

Susan owns a large catering company. She is not married, though she does have a significant other. She doesn't plan to have children. Her ability to be flexible with her time has aided her success as a business owner. She is free to attend almost any event that her company caters, and this personal attention has won over her clients. She spends a lot of time with her nieces and nephews, and every weekend she volunteers with an animal shelter, walking homeless dogs through the city. She loves her career choice, and the nature of her business allows her to interact with an amazing variety of people.

CHOOSING BOTH CAREER AND FAMILY:

Julie

Knowing that she wanted both a career and a family, Julie fully considered her future husband's career path as she planned her own career. Always a planner, Julie went to a small liberal arts college and worked hard, gaining entry to a top law school. While in law school, she specialized in the field of health law, as her husband-to-be planned a career as a neurosurgeon. Julie banked on the fact that her husband would work at a large research hospital and that positions in health law would be abundant nearby. She successfully worked in the field for years. After the birth of her second child, Julie took a four-year hiatus from work. Facing re-entry to the job market and increased responsibility at home, Julie opted to launch her own business, a neurosurgery recruiting firm. Her advice to young pre-professional women is to be practical and flexible when deciding on a career path. She points to "childcare" as a difficult hurdle.

"How can I make a life with this guy I love and raise children who are happy and have their needs met?" Julie has achieved financial success and a fulfilling family life. She found a way to translate her passion into something that she could manage from home. She did not want to give up her career goals, deeply valuing the financial security of a stable second income.

Jenna

Jenna was a graphic design student and married after college. When she had children, she knew that she wanted to continue working. She saw some office space available two blocks from her house, and she opened a nail salon. The salon thrives as a networking spot for women from all walks of life. Jenna makes enough extra income to help her family function with financial ease. She is incredibly happy with the balance that she has in her life: she works her schedule around her children's schedules and she can always close the shop in the event of an emergency at home. Jenna has wonderful support from her husband and family nearby, so she never has to rely on outsiders for childcare. She attributes her happiness to strong relationships with her clients, loving the creativity and personal interaction of her work, and being able to work without compromising her time with her children.

Katie

Katie, now vice president of artistic production for an international music publisher, convinced her company to set up a "home office" in her new Florida home when her physician husband got an opportunity for a better job outside of his native Ohio. She promised the company that her production would not suffer. She had always managed her home with the help of a full-time nanny for her two little girls. Once she moved to Florida, she was hesitant to hire a new nanny.

Eight years later, her home office can be called a success. She has maintained her position as vice president of the company. She travels back to the home office to "check in" with the company for quarterly meetings. Her two daughters often accompany her on these trips to visit grandparents and other family in Ohio. She credits the company's flexibility with its location; in a midsize Midwestern town, the company chose to keep her rather than retrain new talent. She kept her word and maintained their trust with the excellence of her work. The company now allows a variety of employees to manage their work from home offices.

Jan

Jan is a marketing vice president of a huge, international advertising agency. She has worked in advertising since graduating from business school twenty-five years ago. She has successfully raised four boys while working full time and feels fortunate for both her job and family. Being organized is one important feature of Jan's life. Moreover, she focuses on the task at hand, whether it is work or home. "I'm not afraid to ask for help or to hire help when necessary," she says. Although Jan's husband works, his schedule has a lot of flexibility. This factor has also been important in making their lives easier. As her boys have gotten older, Jan feels that the balancing act has gotten easier.

PROS AND CONS – STAY-AT-HOME MOMS:

Women who choose to stay home full time say that one strong "pro" is that you are there for each and every milestone your children reach. Nurturing day in and day out, you never regret having to miss a first tooth, a first step, and the first word. Being the primary caregiver allows you to be nurse, psychologist, social worker, chauffeur, and above all, instiller of family values. Many women clearly glory in the joys of day-to-day motherhood, having the luxury of time to fully enjoy reading, sports, museums, parks, and social activities with family and friends, without time constraints.

In order to stay intellectually stimulated, many stay-at-home moms report that they seek opportunities to be involved in volunteer work, the PTA, and religious and athletic activities. Interviewees also mentioned participation in political campaigns, Big Brother/Big Sister programs, pet shelters, and sports teams. Other stay-at-home moms volunteer their professional expertise to organizations ranging from legal, medical, and accounting to strategic planning and marketing. Some women take classes or join trade associations to keep current in their educational fields.

The stay-at-home moms report several "cons." The most commonly mentioned drawback is the isolation of being at home, particularly with infants and small children. Those who participate in playgroups tend to feel more connected to other women during this phase of childhood development. Without an outlet, many women feel confined at home. Other interviewees mention feeling disconnected from working spouses. Many express regrets at having shortened their careers, placing their own career goals on hold. Many also report diminished self-esteem and some discomfort when relating to women who have maintained or pursued careers.

Overall, our research concludes that many women who stay at home do experience a sense of fulfillment at having such a major impact on the development of their children. Many women have found time for intellectual fulfillment through volunteer work, educational endeavors, religious involvement, fitness, and community activities. Most of the interviewees recommend developing and maintaining relationships with other stay-at-home moms, as the camaraderie enhances their child-focused schedules.

PROS AND CONS – EARLY CAREER FOCUS:

We interviewed several women who followed an early career focus, forging a career without children. These women report high job satisfaction and confidence from financial independence. These women, however, do report experiencing some gaps in emotional fulfillment. To combat these gaps, they say they put a lot of time and energy into community, family, and philanthropic opportunities.

COLLECTIVE ADVICE FROM WOMEN IN THE TRENCHES – THINGS TO CONSIDER WHEN MAKING EARLY LIFE CHOICES:

Here are some considerations to add to your mix of information as you contemplate your career path as a young woman. Combining the goals of work and family presents special challenges, and although the specifics of your situation may not always work out the way you wish, it's wise to think ahead and plan some viable options and possibilities. Whatever direction you may take, if it involves a spouse, that spouse will definitely play a role in meeting the demands of work and family.

1. Think through the childcare issue. Women choosing to have both careers and children at the same time report that one of the biggest challenges is finding consistent,

reliable childcare. When a family member is available to help take care of a sick child, for example, there is a huge sense of relief. For many women, this particular family member may change from year to year. Thus the hurdle of childcare is often an ongoing concern. When considering where you settle, there is a strong case for being near close family and friends.

2. Consider the options and parameters of your potential career choice. Do some research to determine whether this career choice can be translated into something that you can potentially do from home or, at a minimum, on your own schedule. Some of the women we interviewed used their skill sets to find a new application to pursue from home. Other women turned to flex-time work schedules to accommodate the needs of a growing family.

3. How important to me is the idea of financial self-sufficiency? Only you can answer this question. Ask friends, family, and mentors the significance of the issue of money in a relationship and then take this information to ponder how this issue may impact your own future.

4. Am I willing to work for someone else if this dictates that I must compromise time spent with my own family? As every woman we interviewed suggested, if you are your own boss, you can make many of your own decisions.

5. Am I willing to choose a career that may not be a dream but will create a happier reality?

6. Know your priorities and those of your significant other.

However your own path unfolds, you should always take note of the women that have gone before you. At any time, you may reassess your goals, change your path, re-evaluate your opportunities, and follow a new direction. Our advice is to do some thinking now, in order to give yourself more options for your future. Have some deep discussions with your significant other and try to clarify what kind of lifestyle is most appealing to you as a couple. How will your choices affect your responsibilities at home? Will your partner agree to share the burden of domestic responsibilities if you're both working full-time? Does your partner agree to hire help or ask for support from family members? If on the other hand you choose to stay at home or work part-time, is your partner willing to assume the responsibilities as the breadwinner?

The key to your happiness will depend largely upon setting realistic expectations and mutually agreed upon responsibilities. Be intellectually honest about what will bring YOU the most pleasure—having a career, having a family, or striving to combine both? One helpful strategy is to actually write them down on paper so that you can actually visualize which side is dominant. Once you have weighed the pros and cons, you'll have a better chance of laying the foundation for a happy life.

One unifying statement of all the women we interviewed was that they did not regret any time spent at home. "Any time spent with your child is never wasted," one poignantly stated. In the long run, women don't report being highly unsatisfied with putting careers on hold in order to raise a family. This small sampling of women is not meant to cover the entire spectrum of experiences that women across the country may report. Other women are your greatest resource, and you should learn from their mistakes, follow in their triumphs, and ask their advice. Once again, it pays to be proactive.

There is encouraging news for young women motivated to succeed in the workplace. Worldwide, business leaders are recognizing that some women have a particular management style and aptitude for corporate success that some men don't have. According to several studies, some women are particularly strong in a collaborative approach to business, with a matrix structure rather than a traditional hierarchy. In fact, some of the world's most successful women are, or have been, heads of companies such as Areva (nuclear energy), AngloAmerican (mining), Archer Daniels Midland (agribusiness), DuPont (chemicals), Sunoco (oil), and Xerox (technology).

What should be encouraging to young women everywhere is that women are breaking through many, many glass ceilings. Another encouraging trend may be in the types of careers that women are seeking; in 1966, 40 percent of American women who received bachelor of arts degrees specialized in education, with only 2 percent specializing in business and management. In contrast, some current studies report that 50 percent of American women receiving BAs are in business and management, with only 12 percent in education. It's not that educators aren't valuable; the message is that women are no longer confined to that one area.

Women are trending toward making up more and more of the workforce. The Bureau of Labor Statistics states that women make up more than one-third of employees in the areas that are expected to see the greatest job growth in the next decade. Some predict that by 2011, there will be 2.6 million more women than men in American colleges and universities.

On a global scale, the corporate community is starting to address the career/family dilemma. Many elite companies are rethinking their practices in terms of how they determine promotions and partnership. Flexible working options have become important worldwide, with more companies judging workers on annul rather than weekly hours, where late starts and early finishes are tolerated, and where job sharing and telecommuting are options. For example, almost half of Sun Microsystems's employees work from home or nearby satellite offices. Some firms have adopted a network model, where management sees to it that all clients are immediately served, as network members only take work desired. These firms are not necessarily reacting to the situation to be altruistic; instead, there is an amenability to accommodate women because women are proving to be an integral, enhancing part of the new workforce.

As recent studies note, women will soon become the majority of the American workplace. Women work for others, but they are also taking the reins themselves. Women-owned companies in America have increased twice as fast as those owned by men. One of the largest social changes of our times, the economic empowerment of women should inspire and energize all young women of this generation.

FLEXTIME - YOUR BOSS MIGHT BE MORE FLEXIBLE THAN YOU THINK:

Another distinguishing factor in today's workplace is a relatively new phenomenon called flextime. Unlike many of your parents who seem perfectly happy to sit in their cubicles from 9 a.m. to 5 p.m. each day, tirelessly typing away at their computers, many of today's young workers are looking for more flexible schedules. Young workers are constantly on the go, mobile, busy, wired, and oftentimes pulled in many directions. Sound familiar? A flexible work schedule could come in handy. You might be surprised that many employers are looking for the same thing—flexible employees.

We're entering an age of flexible employment, which could become the very cornerstone of our future economy. With so many companies struggling to cut costs to stay afloat, creating flexible work schedules has become a way for companies to cut costs without having to cut employees. In some cases, this means fewer hours for you and, therefore, less money for you. It could also translate into the loss of health care and pension benefits. But before we jump on the "for" or "against" bandwagon about flextime, it's important that we know exactly what it is, as well as what it may mean for your future.

One aspect of work that is rapidly changing is the flexibility of employers to accommodate different work schedules. This is a brand new aspect of the job hunting and interview process. So pay attention to this next section! Chances are that you will encounter at least a few flextime jobs in your search, and knowing the options that are increasingly available will help you determine what kind of flexibility your dream life requires.

WHY SHOULD I CONSIDER A FLEXTIME JOB?

Let's suppose that you're interviewing for a job that advertises itself as a flextime position. What does that mean? What are the advantages for you, the employee?

There are actually several reasons that flextime can be a great idea. In many cases, flextime schedules allow you to spend more time at home or to start earlier in the day (maybe at 7 a.m. instead of 9 a.m.) in order to get home before the sun starts to set.

For parents, flextime allows them to get home around the same time their kids get out of school. It also can mean more savings on daycare for younger children, an expense that seems to always be growing. Taking advantage of a flextime position could mean that a person only works four days a week instead of five and therefore saves money on daycare bills as well as the costs of commuting that day with time left over to work out or meet friends for coffee. As you consider a career, inquire whether a flexible schedule may be available to you in later years should you wish to begin a family.

It's important to keep in mind that flextime options are usually put into effect to save companies money, so it usually works best when the employee is willing to take less money in exchange for having more personal time. If the flextime option includes the loss of health benefits, see if you can be covered under another family member's plan.

If so, forfeiting those benefits can give you more leverage in negotiating a flextime schedule. It's vitally important to know how your concessions will impact the overall value of your job.

TYPES OF FLEXIBLE EMPLOYMENT:

In general terms, flexible employment can mean anything that falls outside of the traditional 9–5 office work hours. It can include changes to the flexibility of hours, scheduling, and shift swapping to a more formal, clearly defined plan that states how much work is, for example, done at home and how employees may withdraw vacation time for more flexibility.

Here are some variations of flextime arrangements that can be seen popping up in companies all across the country:

- Vacation, Work Leave: This includes paid or unpaid leaves for sabbaticals, family, health, or continuing education. This can take the form of purchased "time off," workday "time off" increments, a personal "time off" bank (where it's none of your boss's business why you're requesting off), personal leave, or sick leave.

- Part-time Work Variations: With this, you would agree to a reduction in the number of hours you work, which would result in a lower paycheck, but without any penalty to your benefits. In most cases, your workload should be reduced without any penalty to your job status. This can also include traditional part-time options as well as newer job-sharing between employees (with hours and salary prorated); also, work sharing plans to avoid layoffs during those inevitably slow times of the fiscal year.

- Full-time Flexibility: This can take on many different shapes: seasonal flextime, splitting hours of work done at the office and at home, earlier or later start times or work week compression, such as working four 10-hour days, three 12 hour days, or even 80 hours worked over nine days, with the tenth day free.

HOW DO I GET THIS FLEXIBILITY WITH MY JOB?

Well, before approaching an employer about flexibility options, it's important to have a game plan that demonstrates why a flextime schedule would be good for the company. According to Dr. Kim Cameron, professor of management and organization at the University of Michigan, "When firms can deliver the message that their employees are human resources rather than human costs or liabilities, they see higher profitability, productivity, quality, customer satisfaction, and employee loyalty over the long term." Flextime schedules can produce both a happier employee as well as a happier employer. The old maxim "a happy wife makes for a happy wife" can certainly be applied to the employer-employee relationship.

Here's another way of thinking about it: your written proposal for some sort of flexible employment needs to articulate how the plan benefits the company. This is the key to getting more flexibility in your schedule. Show them how it makes you a better, more productive employee. Your proposal should address all of the implications of the schedule change, both for you and the employer. Here are a few things to include in your written proposal for flextime options:

- Provide details on exactly the kind of flexibility you're proposing
- Tie in your proposal (and relate it) to the company's mission statement (brownie points!)
- Mention the process as one of innovation for the company
- Suggest a trial period of a few months, showing your concern for the plan's effectiveness—make it a specific amount of time (ex: two months)
- Make note of any savings for the company (salary, benefits, etc.) that the flextime plan would include (although you do not necessarily have to give up any of these)
- Mention any previous experience that shows your productivity with a flexible schedule
- Define how the proposal will be assessed and who is necessary for the approval
- Clarify who can terminate the arrangement and what this will result in (maybe a return to the regular schedule?)
- If you're interested in a promotion in the future, outline how the flextime arrangement will affect your progress (in a positive way, right? Explain.)
- Make it clear who will assess how the new schedule is working and how that success will be evaluated

A proposal that includes the above information will knock their socks off and show them that you mean business. You will present yourself as a vital member of the company who is looking for a way to increase productivity and who has thought extensively about how to make a flextime schedule work. In short, you'll look professional, smart, and totally worth the company's investment in you as an employee.

HAMMERING OUT A CONTRACT:

Employment recruiters suggest that people who have been working for some time and are interviewing for a new job should be candid about their compensation expectations in the interview. This discussion typically comes up during the time you are securing the contract with the firm. Let the company share their compensation number first if possible. Since many companies verify prior compensation, be honest about your expected compensation. The key to effective job offer negotiations is effective planning and the use of specific strategy to get what you want. Key points to remember when preparing your negotiating strategy:

- Determine the financial parameters of the job (i.e. salary range and potential bonus payout)
- Research and understand what you are worth in today's marketplace (nationally, regionally, and within the local market in which the employer is situated)
- Assess the competitive environment in which you are competing (i.e. the number of other qualified candidates the company in interviewing)
- Determine the employer's urgency to fill the position
- Use interview feedback to determine the employer's level of interest in hiring you
- Consider cost-of-living differential (new vs. old location), and calculate a break-even salary (based on you current compensation level)

- Consider all out-of-pocket moving expenses (if relocation is required)

In the past, the image of the corporate ladder was dominant: You moved either up or down in a company and those were your only two choices. Many businesses are abandoning this antiquated business model to adopt a lattice approach to career paths, meaning that employees can move side to side and take different avenues to achieve mobility in the company. This is partially a response to your generation, often dubbed the millennial, which insists on more control over schedules in order to balance life with work.

When looking for a job, think about how flextime could improve the quality of your life. It certainly isn't for everyone, but people in many situations could benefit from these sorts of arrangements.

Many thanks to the dozens of career people, career coaches, journalists, students, and administrators who opened their doors to us and shared their valuable insights for the preparation of this book.

For more information on the contents of this book, please contact:

Beth Kuhel bethkuhel@gmail.com

Follow her on Twitter @BethKuhel

Mauri Artz mauriartz@sbcglobal.net

Bibliography

Introduction to Parents

Gibbs, Nancy. "The Case Against Over-Parenting: Why Mom and Dad Need to Cut the Strings." *Time* 30 November 2009. Web.

STEP 1

Cheney, Alexandra. "Firms Assess Young Interns 'Potential.'" *Wall Street Journal* 13 September 2010: B10. Print.

Fiske, Edward B. *The Fiske Guide to Colleges.* (Sourcebooks Inc. 2009).

Gutner, Toddi. "Graduating With a Major in Go-Getting." *Wall Street Journal* 31 March 2009: D6. Print.

McManus, Sean. "Figuring Out What You Want to Do." *Gradspot.com* 11 August 2008. Web. 17 March 2009.

Merritt, Jennifer. "Employers Favor State Schools for Hires." *Wall Street Journal* 13 September 2010: A1. Print.

Mrosko, Terri. "The Difference Between a 'Career' and a 'Job.'" *Cleveland Plain Dealer* 4 October 2009. Print.

Shellenbarger, Sue. "Getting From At-Home To On-The-Job, Even Now." *Wall Street Journal* 29 July 2009: D1. Print.

STEP 2

Barry, Tom. "Health Care Industry is less Affected by Recession." *Atlanta Business Chronicle* 11 January 2002. Print.

"Emerging Industries." *Arreorvoyages.gov* nd. 31 March 2009. Web.

Fendelander, Karl. "From the Ashes: Top Careers in Post Recession America." *Yahoo Education.* n.d. 7 March 2009. Web.

"Fine Print: Funding Priorities and Targeted Savings." *Wall Street Journal* 9 May 2009: A9. Print.

Fitzpatrick, Laura. "We're Getting Off the Ladder." *Time* 25 May 2009. Print.

"Fortune 100 Best Companies to Work for in 2007." *CNNMoney.com.* Web.

Gunter, Toddi. "With Scant Jobs, Grads Make Their Own." *Wall Street Journal Online* 22 December 2009. Web. 23 December 2009.

Hodge, Nick. "Wind Energy Companies." *Greenchipstocks.com* 25 August 2008. Web. 11 March 2009.

Huntsman, Mark. "Staying Power: 5 Careers with Bright Futures." *Yahoo Hotjobs.* n.d. 2 March 2009. Web.

Hyman, Gabby. "Career That Can Fight Recession." *Yahoo Education* n.d. 2 January 2009. Web.

Krizman, Greg. "Product Design and Engineering are Manufacturing Careers with a Bright Future." *Cleveland Plain Dealer* 8 July 2009: F1. Print.

Mrosko, Terri. "Working as an Intern Prepares You for the Right Career." *Cleveland Plain Dealer* 11 October 2009. Print.

"Workplace Trends for 2009." *Cleveland Plain Dealer* 14 January 2009: F1. Print.

Needleman, Sarah E. "Where Stimulus Jobs Will be – And Jobs Open Now." *Wall Street Journal Online.* 25 Feb 2009. Web. 24 March 2009.

Nemko, Marty. "15 Hot Jobs in a (Gulp!) Depression." *US News.com* 27 October 2008. Web. 22 December 2008.

Shellenbarger, Sue. "Weighing the Value of that College Diploma." *Wall Street Journal* 4 November 2009. Print.

"The 10 Recession Proof Companies that are Not Laying Off Workers." *Yahoo News* n.d. 1 April 2009. Web.

"Ten Hottest Careers for College Graduates." *Collegboard. com* n.d. 14 August 2008. Web.

"The 30 Best Careers, 2009's Grades on the Selection Criteria," *USNews.com,* 11 December 2008. Web. 22 December 2008.

Victory, Joy. "10 Hot Professions for 2009." *Yahoo Hotjobs* 13 January 2009. Web.

Wolgemuth, Liz. "The 30 Best Careers for 2009." *Usnews. com* 11 Dec 2008. Web. 1 May 2009.

Zupek, Rachel. "Recession Proof Sectors." *Careerbuilder. com.* Web.

STEP 3

Florida, Richard. "Who's Your City? How the Creative Economy is Making Where to Live the Most Important Decision of Your Life," (Basic Books 2008).

"Forbes Ranks Best Places for Business and Careers." Metro Atlanta Chamber of Commerce. Web.

"2009 10 Best Cities List: It's All About the Jobs!" Martin Prosperity Institute. Web.

"Best Places to Work in the Federal Government." Best-placestowork.org n.d. 8 March 2009. Web.

Badenhausen, Kurt. "The Best States for Business and Careers." Forbes.com 20 October 2010. Web.

Bandy K. M. "The 7 Best States to Start a Business." Usnews.com 6 January 2009. Web. 27 May 2009.

Bernstein, Elizabeth. "Moving Time and Feeling is Queasy." Wall Street Journal Online 28 July 2009. Web. 30 July 2009.

Cooper, Rachel. "Largest Employers in the Washington, D.C. Area." About.com. Web.

Denver Office of Economic Development 2009. Web.

Dresang, Joel. "Forbes ranks Milwaukee in Top 10 Cities for Young Professionals." 15 July 2008. Web.

Dougherty, Conor. "'Youth Magnet' Cities Hit Midlife Crisis." Wall Street Journal 16–17 May 2009: D4. Print.

"Fortune 500." CNNMoney.com. Web.

"Fortune Once Again Names Boston One of Top Ten Best Cities for Business." Boston Redevelopment Committee. Web.

"Full City Rankings 2009." Bureau of Labor Statistics, U.S. Census Bureau, Martin Prosperity Institute. Web.

Georgia Department of Economic Development Official Business Website. 2009. Web.

Grimes, Melanie. "The Best Companies to Work For in Seattle." *Helium.com* Web.

Hedding, Judy. "Best Companies to Work for in the Valley of the Sun." *About.com* Web.

"Highest Paying Jobs in Arizona." *About.com.* Web.

Hill, Catey. "Forbes Best Cities for Jobs in 2009." *Daily News.* Web.

Kaihla, Paul. "Ten Cities Ready to Bounce Back." *CNNMoney.com.* Web.

Kelly, Elizabeth. "The Best Companies to Work for in Seattle." Web.

"Kiplinger's Complete City Rankings for 2009: See How Your City Ranks." *Kiplinger.com* n.d. 28 June 2009. Web.

Lahart, Justin. "Recession's Grip Eases in Parts of Nation." *Wall Street Journal Online* n.d. 11 June 2009. Web.

Lebeau, Raven. *Zillow.com.* Web.

"The Best Companies to Work for in Seattle," *Helium.com.* Web.

"North Texas Boasts 25 Fortune 500 Companies, Up from 2008." North Texas Commission. Web.

Pruitt, Jenny and Associates, Realtors. "13 Georgia Companies in 2009 Fortune 500 List." *Atlanta Business Chronicle* 13 April 2009. Web.

Radnosfsky, Lois. "Washington Firms Soak Up Stimulus." *Wall Street Journal* 17 September 2010. Print.

Scordo, Vincent. "10 Best Cities for New College Grads." *Scordo.com*. 22 April 2009. Web.

"Seattle Cultural Tourism." Seattle's Convention and Visitors Bureau. 5 May 2009. Web.

"The Revival of Pittsburgh: Lessons for the G20." *The Economist* 19 September 2009. Web. 20 September 2009.

Thomas, Scott. "Durham, Raleigh Rank High in Keeping Jobs." *Triangle Business Journal*. Web.

Weiss, Tara. "In Pictures, 10 Cities Where They're Hiring." Web.

Yen, Hope. "Economic Woes Slowing Growth in Sun Belt Region." *Columbus Ledger-Enquirer* 21 March 2009: A13. Print.

STEP 4:

"About Us." *LinkedIn.com*. n.d. 2008. Web.

Buhl, Larry. "6 Soft Skills that could Land You the Job." *Yahoo Hotjobs* n.d. Web. 3 March 2009.

"College Grads face Worst Job Market in Years." *USA Today* 3 April 2009. Web.

Cheney, Alexandra. "Firms Assess Young 'Interns' Potential." *Wall Street Journal* 13 September 2010: B10. Print.

Decker, Andy. "Writing a Recession-Proof Resume." *Atlantawomanmag.com* 9 January 2009. Web. 27 January 2009.

Evans, Teri. "Research Agreements Play Big Role in Jobs," *Wall Street Journal.* 13 September 2010: B8. Print.

Hofferber, Karen. "5 Ways to Recession-Proof Your Resume." *Resumepower.com* 5 December 2008. Web. 27 January 2009.

Isaacs, Kim. "What's Your Resume Objective?" *Monster. com.* Web.

Mrosko, Terri. "Working as an Intern Prepares You for the Right Career." *Cleveland Plain Dealer* 11 October 2009. Print.

Needleman, Sarah. "Creating a Resume That Sells." *Wall Street Journal Online* 24 November 2009. Web. 1 December 2009.

"Giving a Stalled Job Search a Jump-Start." *Wall Street Journal* 20 October 2009. Print.

Nemko, Marty. "Ahead-Of-the-Curve Careers." *Yahoo Hotjobs.* n.d. 22 December 2008. Web.

Shellenbarger, Sue. "Getting From At-Home to On-the-Job, Even Now." *Wall Street Journal Online* 29 July 2009. Web. 30 July 2009.

Tomasula, Tom Jr. "Help Me Help You...The Best Practices for Working with a Corporate Recruiter to Land your Next Position." *Cleveland Plain Dealer* 11 November 2009. Print.

Yang, Jia Lynn. "How to Get a Job When No One's Hiring." *CNNMoney.com.* 31 March 2009. Web.

Zaslow, Jeffrey. "The Greatest Generation of Networkers." *Wall Street Journal* 4 November 2009: D1. Print.

Zernika, Kate. "Making College Relevant." *New York Times* 29 December 2009. Web. 4 January 2010.

"ZoomInfo.com Unveils New Site with Free Company Profiles." *Infotoday.com.* 9 April 2007. Web. 28 April 2009.

Evans, Teri. "Research Agreements Play Big Role in Jobs." *Wall Street Journal.* 13 September 2010. B8. Print.

STEP 5

Hovanec, Eric. "Mastering the Informational Interview." *Yahoo.com* n.d. 22 December 2008. Web.

Lubline, Joann. "Talking Too Much on a Job Interview May Kill Your Chance." *Wall Street Journal Online* 30 October 2007. Web. 18 November 2009.

Needleman, Sarah. "Giving a Stalled Job Search a Jump-Start." *Wall Street Journal* 20 October 2009: D8. Print.

"Making a Match: Job Sites Get Personal." *Wall Street Journal* 9 July 2009: D2. Print.

Porter, Jane. "Unleashing Your Creativity While You're Moonlighting." *Wall Street Journal* 3 November 2009: D6. Print.

Weiss, Tara. "Landing Your First Job." *Forbes.com* 26 April 2007. Web.

Zaslow, Jeffrey. "Advice on Giving Advice to 20-Year-Olds." *Wall Street Journal.* 1 September: 2010, D1, D2. Print.

For Girls Eyes' Only

Alsop, Ronald. "Parental Controls." *Wall Street Journal* 30 September 2006: R4. Print.

Bowers, Katherine. "How Women Lawyers are Reaching Greater Heights with Fewer Billable Hours." Web.

"Female Power." *The Economist* 2 January 2010: 49–51. Print.

"Lessons from the Trenches: Learning from $1 Million Plus Entrepreneurs." Center for Women's Business Research. 2008. Web.

Ho, Janie. "The Return of the MBA Mom." *Business Week* 11 May 2006. Web. 14 May 2007.

Marr, Melissa. "50 Women to Watch." *Wall Street Journal* 10 November 2009. Print.

Okoben, Janet. "Stimulus Money Created Job for Her." *Cleveland Plain Dealer* 2 August 2009: B3. Print.

Palanjan, Amy. "Tap Existing Skills, Old Ties When Changing Your Career." *Wall Street Journal* 8 April 2008: D4. Print.

Schweitzer, Karen. "U.S. Women's Business Organizations." *About.com.* Web.

Shellenbarger, Sue. "Have a Nice Midlife Crisis." *Wall Street Journal Online* 22 December 2009. Web. 23 December 2009.

Shin, Annys. "Career or Family? Yes." *Washington Post* 22 March 2008. Web. 13 September 2008.

"Stand Up for Flex." *Working Mother* Oct. 2009: 63–74. Print.

Stark, Mallory. "Women Find New Path to Work." *hbswk. hbs.edu* 15 May 2006. Web. 14 May 2007.

Story, Louise. "Many Women at Elite Colleges Set Career Path to Motherhood." *New York Times Online* 20 September 2005. Web.

"Thinking About Re-Entering the 9-5 World? Want Help?" *www.3babson.edu* 5 August 2006. Web. 14 May 2007.

"We Did It! The Rich World's Quiet Revolution: Women are Gradually Taking Over the Workplace." *The Economist* 2 January 2010: 7. Print.

"Womenomics." *The Economist* 2 January 2010: 48. Print.

"Women Who Step Out of the Corporate World Find it Hard to Step Back In." September 2005. Web. 14 May 2007.

Working Mother October 2009. Print.

Other Useful Websites:

www.zoominfo.com

www.indeed.com

www.newscom.com

www.flexpaths.com

www.on-ramps.com (NYC)

www.workoptions.com

www.flexperience.com (San Francisco)

www.flexibleresources.com (Stanford, CT)

www.flexwork.com (CA)

www.flexibleexecutives.com (Atlanta)

www.careerpartners.com (CA)

www.jobshareconnection.com (FL)

www.myparttimepro.com (NYC, Washington, DC, PA)

www.needlestackjobs.com (National, based in OH)

www.monster.com

www.careerbuilder.com

www.metrodenver.org

www.citydata.com

www.metromsp.org

Although this book is not a guide for starting your own business, the option of being an entrepreneur is certainly worth mentioning. Below is a list of valuable resources if this is the path you wish to travel. Many beginning entrepreneur books have been published in the past few decades and can be found online or in your local bookstore.

Association of Collegiate Entrepreneurs (ACE)

ACE is an international organization that enables students to operate small business ventures and interact with other aspiring entrepreneurs.

College Startup

A blog with helpful information and advice for entrepreneurs in college

Collegiate Entrepreneurs' Organization (CEO)

The Collegiate Entrepreneurs' Organization encourages college students to seek opportunity through enterprise creation. It also offers excellent networking and information resources, including three annual conferences.

Consortium for Entrepreneurship Education

Site provides information on small business design and management, micro-enterprise, home-based business, self-employment, and basic business start up.

Energizing Young Entrepreneurs

A project of the RUPRI Center for Rural Entrepreneurship, the site provides resources for young entrepreneurs, particularly those living in rural communities. It also conducts a talent search and seeks to highlight successful young, rural business owners.

Entrepreneur U

Sponsored by the Ewing Marion Kauffman Foundation, this site provides information and resources for teachers and students that emphasize the importance of entrepreneurship. It also provides a comprehensive listing of scholarships.

Ewing Marion Kauffman Foundation

The Kauffman Foundation has resources and programs for youth and collegiate level entrepreneurs. It also has an Entrepreneurship Internship Program (KEIP), which immerses students in the day-to-day reality of starting and managing a business.

Future Business Leaders of America

Future Business Leaders of America-Phi Beta Lambda is a nonprofit 501(c) (3) educational association of students preparing for careers in business and business-related fields.

Gen-X Idea Café

Idea Café caters to the business needs of Generation X entrepreneurs with information and advice to feed both mind and business. The site also includes inspirational stories of successful young entrepreneurs.

Global Student Entrepreneur Awards

Presented by Mercedes-Benz, the GSEA Program awards $100,000 in cash, business products, and services to student entrepreneurs and is a great opportunity to obtain start-up funding.

Ideas for Young Entrepreneurs Blog

This blog provides frequently updated ideas, advice, and information for young entrepreneurs.

Inc.'s Young Entrepreneur's Survival Kit

Inc. has collected profiles of business owners who started their businesses while students, along with resources related to building a business, links to academic programs, and ideas on networking with peers.

Independent Means Inc.

A provider of products and services for youth financial independence, this site offers know-how on starting a business as well as making, saving, giving, and growing money. The site also holds an annual business plan competition with a $1,000 cash prize.

Internal Revenue Service (IRS)

The IRS has an online workshop for young people to help them understand the why and how of meeting their tax obligations. They also provide free products for small businesses and self-employed persons.

JA Titan 3.0

A fun and interactive game in which visitors can test their skills running a business in this ultimate business simulation. Players are CEOs who must run a manufacturing company and master six key business decisions.

Junior Achievement (JA)

Junior Achievement seeks to educate and inspire young people to value free enterprise, business, and economics in order to better prepare them for their future.

McKelvey Foundation

The McKelvey Foundation awards a total of $40,000 in scholarships annually for young entrepreneurs to attend any four-year college in the United States.

Mind Petals: Young Entrepreneur Network

Mind Petals is a young entrepreneur's blog and networking site that produces informative and inspiring content. This entrepreneurial-focused community seeks to instill ambition, motivation, and alternate ways of thinking.

Mind Your Own Business

Sponsored by the SBA and Junior Achievement, this site is designed to support interest in entrepreneurship among teens. It serves as a small business portal for young entrepreneurs by providing essential resources and information.

National Collegiate Inventors and Innovators Alliance (NCIIA)

The NCIIA is an alliance of faculty and students working to advance invention and innovation in higher education. Its mission is to nurture a new generation of innovators by promoting curricula to teach creativity, invention, and entrepreneurship.

Prudential Young Entrepreneurs Program

PYEP is an entrepreneurial development and job creation strategy for entrepreneurs ages eighteen to thirty who reside in Newark, N.J., and Philadelphia, Pa.

Renegade CEOs

The Renegade CEOs community provides teen entrepreneur resources and a variety of products, people, and services that encourage teens to manifest their raw talent in a "global living laboratory."

SBA's Teen Business

This site offers information on starting a business—from brainstorming and evaluating the feasibility of your idea to developing a business plan and making sound financial decisions. It also includes interactive games and motivational success stories.

SBA's Young Entrepreneurs

A comprehensive list of SBA-sponsored online resources for young entrepreneurs. Information is available for young children up to young adults.

Starve Ups

A non-profit entrepreneurial support organization dedicated to helping entrepreneurs create and sustain successful businesses. The organization sponsors business and networking events and also provides resources and a job listing.

Streaming Futures

This site allows teens to interact with career professionals through live, monthly interactive webcasts. Its goal is for teenagers to get extensive insight into careers by watching interviews of real industry leaders performing their duties.

Students in Free Enterprise (SIFE)

SIFE is a collegiate, free enterprise organization for students in twenty countries. The organization focuses on five key areas: market economics, success skills, entrepreneurship, financial literacy, and business ethics.

Teen Entrepreneur

An online division of *Entrepreneur* magazine, Teen Entrepreneur provides a wealth of information, advice, motivation, tools, and other resources for young people who are serious about entrepreneurship.

The Mint: Be Your Own Boss

This site provides middle and high school students with helpful advice, interactive quizzes, and fun resources related to money management. There is also information specifically for parents and teachers.

Top Ten Small Business Owners Under 16

An inspiring article by LegalZoom highlighting the successes of young entrepreneurs.

United States Hispanic Chamber of Commerce (USHCC) Foundation

USHCC offers a Regional Youth Entrepreneurship "BizFest" for students ages seventeen to twenty-five and also provides scholarships and internship opportunities. Online <u>videos</u> from the "Bizfest" can be viewed from the foundation website.

Young America's Business Trust

A young startup initiative, YABT combines the energy of young people to unleash the entrepreneurial potential of youth. The site also sponsors the <u>Young Entrepreneurs Talent and Innovation Competition of the Americas.</u>

YoungBiz.com

Geared toward teens, the mission of YoungBiz is to empower youth with entrepreneurial, business, and financial skills through innovative education and real-world experience.

Young Entrepreneur Foundation (YEF)

Created by the National Federation of Independent Business, YEF's mission is to educate young people about the critical role of small business and to help students interested in business and entrepreneurship further their education.

Young Entrepreneur's Survival Kit

An online resource center for young entrepreneurs provided by *Inc.* magazine. This section contains expert columns and advice from successful young business owners.

Your Success Network

The goal of this organization is to continuously build and maintain a global community of young business owners and aspiring entrepreneurs, providing a forum where they can share dreams, goals, experiences, and resources.

Online Resources include:

www.business.gov www.sba.gov The small business administration offers resources on how to start a business

www.bizymoms.com Information on starting a business, including home based-businesses

www.morebusiness.com

www.entrepeneur.com Information on starting and running a business

www.smallbusinesscenter.com Covers topics on financing

www.startupnation.com How to start a business *and* keep it going

www.bplans.com Provides five hundred sample business plans

www.businessplans.org Resources to help you write your own business plans, plus samples

www.grants.gov Search government grants

www.sba.gov/smallbusinessplanner/plan/writeabusiness-plan/index.html Walks you through the steps of writing a business plan

Print Resources:

Barrow, Colin. The Business Plan Workbook: The Definitive Guide to Researching, Writing Up and Presenting a Winning Plan, 2008 658.401

Chambers, K. Dennis. The Entrepreneur's Guide to Writing Business Plans and Proposals, 2008 658.4012

Pakroo, Peri. The Small Business Start-Up Kit, 2010 346.0652

Patrow, Donna. Making Money From Home: How to Run a Successful Home-Based Business, 2010. 658.0412

Steingold, Fred. Legal Forms for Starting & Running a Small Business, 2010 346.06520269